Law and Society
Recent Scholarship

Edited by Eric Rise

A Series from LFB Scholarly

The Development Dilemma

The Political Economy of Intellectual Property Rights in the International System

Robert L. Ostergard, Jr.

LFB Scholarly Publishing LLC
New York 2003

Library of Congress Cataloging-in-Publication Data

Ostergard, Robert L.
The development dilemma : the political economy of intellectual property rights in the international system / Robert L. Ostergard, Jr.
p. cm. -- (Law and society)
Includes bibliographical references and index.
ISBN 1-931202-47-8 (alk. paper)
1. Intellectual property--Political aspects--Developing countries. 2. Intellectual property (International law) I. Title. II. Law and society (New York, N.Y.)
K1401 .O84 2002
341.7'58--dc21

2002015790

ISBN 1-931202-47-8

Printed on acid-free 250-year-life paper.

Manufactured in the United States of America.

Contents

Acknowledgements

First, I am grateful for the support provided by the National Science Foundation during completion of the original manuscript. I completed the original manuscript for this book three years ago as the capstone to five and a half years as a graduate student in the Department of Political Science at Binghamton University, State University of New York. Several people during and after my graduate career made this book possible. Foremost amongst them are David Cingranelli and Michael McDonald. David introduced me to the issues surrounding the debates in the intellectual property rights literature during my days as his student. He gave his time freely to me, shaping the ideas and concepts presented in this book. His friendship, commitment, and belief in this project helped get me through the toughest challenges while finishing my graduate studies.

Michael McDonald's influence is on just about every page of this manuscript. Michael has been an incredible driving force during my time at Binghamton University. He, more than most, helped shape my academic and world view. I am truly indebted to Michael as a scholar and as a friend.

After my graduate studies, I found a home at the Institute of Global Cultural Studies (IGCS) at Binghamton University and two incredible friends and colleagues, Ali Mazrui and Ricardo Laremont. Ali Mazrui, the Director of IGCS, gave me my first academic appointment as a post-doctoral fellow, providing me with the tools and resources I needed to start my academic career. Ali gave me early opportunities that no other person could. He has been a phenomenal inspiration professionally and personally for the past three years and now I proudly serve as his Associate Director at IGCS. This book would not have been possible without his commitment and friendship.

Ricardo Laremont, the Associate Director of IGCS during my fellowship, was always available for me. Ricardo is not only an outstanding mentor, but also an extraordinary friend. Ricardo's drive and creativity provided a source of encouragement during his time at IGCS. I owe much to Ricardo both intellectually and personally.

I am also indebted to the staff at IGCS who not only provided support, but a great laugh when needed. Barbara Tierno, Nancy Levis, AnnaMarie "Speedy" Palombara, and Goretti Mugambwa all provided friendship and support during this process.

Of course I am also indebted to friends and family members who tolerated me while completing this project. Bill and Amanda Hollister (the Homus King and Queen of New York), Ron Thompson and Joe Willey were bedrocks of support during this process. My sister Joan certainly made life interesting during this time as well.

Dean Kehoe has been the best friend anybody could want. Possessing an uncanny ability to find humor in the worst of times, Dean was always there to lighten things up a bit. He did not always have answers, but he did what great friends do sometimes—they just listen. Oh yeah, he has some pretty good editing skills that helped, in his words, to "douche" the manuscript for publication. (He provides a great alibi for typographical mistakes made in the manuscript.) I owe much to Dean and will be forever grateful to him. Above all, my Mother and Father, Jean and Robert Ostergard, have always been there for me. Through all the good and bad times, I could always count on them for their love and support. My success is as much a reflection of them as it is of me.

It is to Mom, Dad and Dean that this book is dedicated.

Introduction

In 1994 more than one hundred states signed the Marrakesh Agreement establishing the World Trade Organization (WTO) and the implementation of the Uruguay Round of the General Agreement on Tariffs and Trade (GATT). As a result of a strong lobbying effort by the United States (US) the GATT agreement included a global trade regime for the protection of intellectual property rights (IPR). The agreement bound *all* signatory states to implementing a full Western-style intellectual property (IP) regime within sixteen years of ratification. The agreement itself was the final product of a long process that elevated the IPR issue from an obscure, esoteric legal field to a critical political and economic issue that brought states to the brink of trade wars.

Traditionally, IPR have been the concern of lawyers protecting their client's ideas and discoveries. Economists took notice of the issue following the seminal work of Joseph Schumpeter, who argued that innovation and technology were *the* driving forces behind industrial growth and development (Schumpeter 1976). Economists focused their attention on the importance of IPR to domestic economic growth through mediums such as foreign investment and technology transfers. But with the growing financial strength of transnational corporations (TNCs), the increasingly interdependent nature of the international system, and the globalization of productive processes, the IPR issue acquired significant political and policy overtones, placing it squarely in the realm of political scientists.

Despite the clear political implications of the issue, they can not be separated from the legal and economic issues that surround IPR. Nor should they be. Politics do affect global legal and economic policies and institutions, which is the fundamental premise of this book. Hence, two questions emerge that have propelled this research: *why do states adopt strong intellectual property protection and what are the effects of adopting such policies?* While these questions will be addressed in more detail later, two related issues need attention. The first concerns the motivations for adopting IPR policies. The second pertains to the behavior of different states in the international system.

Economists and lawyers typically have argued that states should adopt strong IPR policies simply because they are beneficial. They promote economic growth, foreign investment, indigenous research, and technology transfer. State behavior was rational if they reasoned that the positive effects of the policy outweighed the negative effects. Economists and legal scholars viewed politics as static, a constant in the pursuit of purely rational economic and legal goals. But by ignoring politics, researchers exposed only part of the modern IPR research agenda.

Why Nations Adopt IPR Protection: The General Framework

This research begins with the assumption that states do not adopt strong IPR policies as a matter of rational *economic* policy only, but also as a matter of rational *political* policy. Economists and legal scholars have argued that nations should adopt strong IPR policies as a matter of promoting economic growth. But the governments of some states perceive the benefits of a weak IPR regime as being greater than the benefits derived from a enacting a strong regime. A weak IPR regime allows states to acquire inexpensive technology by not paying royalties and licensing fees that IPR protection requires in order to use IP. So why would a state adopt policies that are contrary to its perceived interests? Why would a state adopt a strong IPR regime when it is more beneficial to maintain a weak one? In answering this question, the beneficiaries of a strong domestic IPR regime must be explored—industries whose IP is most commonly stolen. If states perceive a weaker domestic and global IPR regime as beneficial to their interests, then the only reason to deter them from this strategy is the demands placed on them by special interests that can make it worthwhile for states to adopt stronger IPR protection.

With regard to interest groups, a few clarifying points are needed. All states are not equal in their level of political and economic development, which means interest groups domestically have different political effects across different states. The type of interest groups and how they operate will vary from one state to the next. Groups and their behavior in the US will be different from those in China or in South Africa. Moreover, not all states are at the same economic development level, which means that certain interest groups are not present in some countries. The influence of the US software and semi-conductor industries is not equivalent to that of the same industries in India or Brazil. Because of the importance of these industries to the US economy, they exert substantial influence on the political process. These conceptions of interest groups in political and economic development portray them as domestic actors that exercise control and influence within the confines of the state. But this limitation must be relaxed to achieve an understanding of the IPR issue.

Interest groups can also be foreign actors such as other states and TNCs. State and non-state actors compete in the international system to achieve goals that may or may not coincide with those of other state and non-state actors. Thus, another premise in this research is that developed states pursue different goals than do developing states and therefore behave differently in the international system. Developed countries have attained a level of economic and political development that provides a high standard of living for their people. Their goal, at minimum, is to maintain that level of development. Developing countries have not attained the same level of economic or political development. Their goals reflect the desire to improve the standard of living for their people. But different forces affect how developed and developing countries pursue these goals. Actors and circumstances that effect behavior at both the domestic and international levels confront both groups of states. But this has not always been recognized in the scholarly literature.

As Haggard (1990) observes, traditionally in international relations theory, two schools of thought governed scholars' interpretations of state action at the international level. The first was the coalitional approach, which focuses on the interests and organizational power of dominant social actors as the source of state action. The second was an institutional approach that viewed policies as the outcome of the preferences of the political, military, and bureaucratic elites. Much has been written on these two approaches, particularly in efforts to show why one approach is better than the other. This avenue of argument has led to redundant literature that has brought us no closer to understanding how states and non-state actors behave in the international system. In fact, both approaches suffer from a myopic, over-simplified interpretation of international events. Often, in the haste to simplify our understanding of the world, we lose sight of important facets that can shed light. Both approaches, when treated exclusively, do this. The coalitional approach views the state hopelessly at the whim of special interest coalitions while the institutional approach leaves out the possibility that the state may indeed respond to groups or individual constituents.

In fact, the state is active in the interplay of two distinct societies: the domestic society and the international society, each possessing forces that influence the state. The state does not operate exclusively in the realm of one *or* the other; instead, the state attempts to temper or to enhance the effect that each society has on the other. The state's role is to filter the extreme demands placed on the two societies by each other without compromising its own security and stability.

For instance, during the 1990s when domestic interest groups called for repeal of China's most-favored nation trade status in the US in protest of its abysmal human rights policies, the Chinese government pressured the US government to maintain its status. The US government's goal was to balance the demands of the domestic interests against Chinese demands in light of the economic and political security issues confronting the US government. Hence, the extreme position of canceling most-favored nation trade status was assuaged to avert a potential trade war with the Chinese that would have significant political and economic security implications. The US government, to meet the demands of domestic interest groups, applied strong diplomatic pressure on China's government to address the human rights issue. While not ideal to either the domestic actors (human rights groups) or the international actor (China), the US government balanced the competing demands to fulfill its security interests.

A state's decision to act is not based on domestic forces only, nor is it based exclusively on international forces. But forces on either side can motivate the state to act contrarily to the forces of the other and possibly even contrarily to security and other interests that may motivate the state. What this model implies is that the state has to consider both domestic and international consequences when deciding to adopt particular policies, such as strong domestic IPR regimes. This point draws immediately back to the developed and developing country differences on the IPR issue and the different forces, domestically and internationally, that affect the decision to adopt a particular level of IPR protection.

Domestically, developing countries and developed countries face different types of pressures when adopting IPR protection suited to their objectives. We might be able to think of this in terms of a development continuum that stretches over time and ranges from the least developed countries to the most developed countries. In presenting this idea, I do not advocate a deterministic, evolutionary path that all states *will* follow on the quest to increase their development (a la Karl Marx or W. W. Rostow). Rather, what I am suggesting is that states that possess particular characteristics at various stages of political and economic development will pursue different IPR policies and that changes in these policies will occur only when either their level of development changes or when domestic or international pressure coerces the state to do so. The two events may or may not be connected. As a state develops politically and economically, interest groups may form that will seek stronger IPR protection. It may also be the case, however, that states that are pursuing strong economic growth and development policies may attract foreign interests seeking to share the financial benefits of the state's strong growth.

For simplicity, states can be divided into three categories of strategic interest in IPR protection based of their current level of political and economic development: least developed, moderately developed and most developed.

Least developed: These states have no incentive to adopt strong IPR protection or to spend the resources needed for enforcing it. Industrial interest groups, particularly those involved in high technology products, either have not formed or are not powerful enough to pressure the government to adopt stronger protection. The government pursues weak protection policies to acquire needed technology that cannot be developed indigenously. Domestic markets are underdeveloped and there is negligible trade with other states. Hence, international pressure to enhance IPR protection is limited, if it exists at all. IPR laws are generally the remnants of colonial laws with some minor enhancements.

Newly developing or moderately developed: The states are entering a stronger economic stage of growth and development characterized by emerging markets and low to moderate technological capacity. They are developing key industries for growth through a combination of targeted trade to enhance revenues and protectionist measures to protect the industries' domestic market. Industries may not seek IPR protection until they become producers of new technology instead of "free-riding" consumers of existing technology. Because of the growth rates or the potential untapped consumer markets, foreign investment and trade seek to exploit new business opportunities. The origins of pressure to expand IPR protection begin here.

Developed: These states have fully developed technological capacities and are on the cutting edge of industrial research and production. They implement the strongest IPR protection and adapts it to accommodate new technologies and processes. Consumer markets are fully developed and oftentimes saturated with products, forcing businesses to explore alternative markets. Governments work closely with business to ensure strong IPR protection in foreign markets. Strong domestic pressure to maintain and to update IPR protection is present, as well as pressures to promote such protection in international markets.

Theoretically, developing countries have little incentive to adopt strong IPR protection policies unless they are met with some form of coercive action either domestically or internationally or through some combination of the two. The goal of the state is to develop an IPR strategy that is suited to its needs while balancing competing demands domestically and internationally.

Internationally, the US has been the leading proponent of the new IPR regime. Because of domestic changes to its industrial base and the rise of global competition, US industry turned to the government to secure overseas protection of its IPR. The government took up this cause, realizing that the US comparative advantage was indeed shifting from manufacturing and agricultural products to those in the high technology sectors that require greater IPR protection. But the US couched this domestic issue in terms of international benefits to be derived from global protection of IPR without regard for where particular countries were in their development process. All countries would benefit from strong IPR, the US government argued. But not all countries agreed that economic growth would result from stronger IPR protection.

Brazil and India's opposition to addressing the IPR protection issue in the GATT forum centered on the debate surrounding the relationship between IPR protection and economic growth. Both governments argued for greater access to technology that would assist in generating economic growth. The governments of developed countries countered this argument, contending that these goals would only come about through more stringent protection of IPR. The US led the charge in this respect by pressuring governments of developing countries into accepting stringent IPR regulations. What the argument leads to is the question: Does strong IPR protection have the effect that the governments of developed countries claim? That is, does strong IPR protection promote economic growth? The evidence presented here explores the economic growth argument and finds little support for the developed countries' claims either theoretically or empirically.

Research Outline

The United Nations Universal Declaration of Human Rights considers the guarantee of IPR to be a human right. This perspective, however, seems to clash with the idea that other rights, such as the right to subsistence and medical care, may conflict with the right to profits inherent in the IPR human rights guarantee. Chapter one establishes a theoretical framework that rejects the United Nations' position on IPR protection, contending that we should not guarantee IPR as human rights in light of the duty to provide for other fundamental needs such as food, medicine and shelter. The notion of universal IPR protection is rejected in favor of a selective approach that prioritizes the goals and objectives that states have. Both theoretical and policy-oriented approaches are established for explaining and justifying why states have different IPR protection policies.

Chapters two and three empirically address the central research questions. Two major concepts are addressed in chapter two. First, the measurement of IPR protection is reassessed and a new measure is constructed which incorporates both the strength of the laws and their enforcement. Next, an empirical analysis of the IPR-economic growth debate is presented using the new IPR protection measures. Little evidence supporting the positive relationship between the two is found. Chapter three uses the new IPR measures to examine why states adopt the IPR protection levels they do. Evidence suggests international and domestic factors play varying roles in determining a state's IPR protection policies based upon the state's development level.

In chapters four, five and six, qualitative research evidence is used to explore the framework and models presented in the introduction and chapters one through three. Case studies of the US, China, and South Africa illustrate the domestic and international pressures that have shaped and influenced IPR protection policies in each country. The case study of the US is an example of the evolution of IPR protection in a developed country as it moves through stages of development. In chapter five, research suggests that China's initial experience with IPR protection was not domestically initiated, but imposed on them by foreign actors. In the modern period, with China's emergence as an economic power, foreign pressure mounted for the government to protect IPR more stringently. This issue led to major trade clashes between the US and China, pushing both countries to the brink of trade wars. Finally, the South Africa case study in chapter six demonstrates the problem developing countries face when they have to choose between strong IPR protection and providing basic services to their people. Confronted with a crippled health care system and the HIV/AIDS epidemic, the government of South Africa faced international opposition when it changed its patent laws to guarantee greater access to anti-AIDS drugs. Pressure from the US and TNCs mounted, putting the South African government on the defense, forcing it to choose between strong IPR protection and basic health services for its people.

Chapter One

A Clash of Interests: Development, Universal Human Rights, and Intellectual Property Rights*

Introduction

Given the ever-widening acceptance of a *right* to protection of intellectual property (IP), one might assume that there is at least implicitly an equally broad and agreed upon rationale or justification for this right. This, however, is not the case. Among those who write on the subject, there are two dominant, and not at all consistent, lines of reasoning. John Locke's labor theory of property, one of the foundations of traditional property rights in the modern world, is a logical starting point for attempts to justify intellectual property rights (IPR), that is, the protection of exclusive ownership in intangible objects that acquire their value mainly from creative efforts. The second justification for IPR is derived from a traditional doctrine of utilitarian inference, whereby the right to property is granted based on maximizing the benefits society can obtain. Although there are zones of overlap between these two lines of reasoning, even if they are taken together and their zones of disagreement ignored, they do not constitute an adequate or coherent prescriptive theory for the recognition of IPR. Without a logical foundation for justifying IPR, their consideration as a basic human right seems untenable. Although the most frequently offered justifications for a right to IP are anchored in relatively modern theoretical arguments, there are substantially older historical precedents for this policy. Intellectual property issues date to the Chinese Zhou dynasty (1122 BCE), when concern arose for commodity identification. By CE 835, the Wenzong Emperor barred the unauthorized reproduction of documents, calendars, and other items related to prognostication (Alford 1995: 13). In the Western world, IPR in the form of patents came into existence around 1500 in Venice and spread to most of the major European powers by 1550, more than a century before John Locke's work on private property. Governments gradually recognized rights that owners had to their ideas. Subsequently, states adapted IPR to accommodate the increasingly expansive growth of technological innovations. In the modern era, however, the claim to IPR has evolved from a state-granted right to a universal human right without substantial scrutiny.

An alternative view of IPR protection needs to be explored: not all IPR should be justified. If we assume that the state's responsibility to provide for people's physical welfare takes precedence over an individual's right to profit, several propositions emerge. The first is that there exists a hierarchy of intellectual objects based on a generally perceived notion of physical welfare. The second is that when discussing IPR, the emphasis must not be exclusively on the rights of producers; IPR must also be examined from the perspective of consumers and the national welfare. Both of these propositions focus on nations' attempts to fulfill their citizens' basic needs, which are largely grounded in technologies and processes that sustain physical well-being. Consequently, if certain individuals have exclusive control of established technologies, other individuals may be deprived of basic products that could contribute to their betterment.

Before elaborating on these arguments, an exploration of the differences between traditional property and IP, as well as the two traditional theories used to justify IPR, is needed. We must also consider the role that IP plays in contributing to people's welfare. Finally, the IP argument set forward here needs to be given some context. The starkest examples of how IP can affect people's welfare are best examined through the prism of North-South relations and the different meaning that IPR has for both groups of countries.

Property Rights and Intellectual Property Theory

Property, in one form or another, has been a concern in many of history's struggles for fundamental rights. The Magna Carta (1215), the US Declaration of Independence (1776), the French Declaration of the Rights of Man and Citizen (1789), and the Universal Declaration of Human Rights (1948) all recognize property rights in some form. Generally, this right to property refers to tangible items, such as land, business establishments, housing, and other resources. Yet there is another form of property, consisting of intangible items such as intellectual objects. The theoretical justification for intangible property has been grounded in two traditional theories: Locke's labor theory of property, and utilitarianism.

John Locke's Labor Theory of Property

John Locke justified property rights through labor. In his view, objects produced by an individual through the mixing of labor with resources are the property of that individual alone. Locke's theory of property also contains two limitations on the acquisition of property. The first is on the amount of property that can be appropriated: "enough and as good left in common for others" (Locke 1988: 290).[1] In other words, so long as others are not made worse off by the acquisition, there is no limit on the amount that may be appropriated. The second limitation relates to the amount of an item that can be used: a person should not take more of an object than can be used before it spoils.

Locke's labor theory of property is problematic, however, when used to justify IPR. In particular, the question of ownership in the cumulative inventive process poses a serious problem. For example, technology that is developed by one person is often employed in new products without ownership privileges being granted to the original inventor. Similarly, literary works often build on the fruits of other efforts. Because their labor is embodied in the new product, are the prior inventors and writers entitled to partial ownership of the object? If past inventors used their labor to create the object, does their right to property diminish if others utilize the product? As these questions suggest, the cumulative process of inventions complicates the question of ownership if labor is used to justify IPR. Therefore, an alternative view of Locke's labor theory is needed.

One of the most frequently cited analyses of Locke's labor theory of property is that of Robert Nozick (1974). Nozick points out that while mixing one's labor with something could bring about ownership of the object, it could also result in a loss of one's labor. That is, why should the act of mixing labor justify the ownership of previously unowned property? He uses the example of pouring juice into the seas and then asking whether now he owns the sea or has lost his juice. Ultimately, Nozick rejects Locke's emphasis on labor in favor of a distribution of property based on Locke's first proviso.

Nozick interprets Locke's first proviso as meaning that others, no longer free to use the appropriated property, should not be made worse off than before the property was appropriated. At the center of the "worse-off" argument is the question: worse off compared to what? Individuals are "worse-off," according to Nozick, if: (1) they lose the opportunity to improve their situation by a particular appropriation; or (2) they are no longer able to use freely what they could previously use. Under a strict interpretation of the "worse-off" condition, when a person has nothing to counter the loss, then the person is "worse-off" under both premises. A weaker interpretation of being "worse-off" would ignore the second premise and be based exclusively on the first. It may be possible, according to Nozick, that although individuals could no longer appropriate an object, they would still be able to use it. Despite this, people would still be "worse-off" because of restrictions on access to the item. Furthermore, he contends that any theory of justice in the acquisition of property must include this second proviso (178).

Nozick further argues that a baseline for the comparison of "worse-off" must be established. For instance, he applies this notion of a baseline directly to intellectual objects, which are ipso facto private property in his scheme (181).[2] He tells the story of a medical researcher who creates a new drug to treat a disease. The researcher refuses to sell the substance unless exclusive individual control over the product is guaranteed. According to Nozick, this situation does not violate the first Lockean proviso. The baseline in this example is the absolute condition of people before the discovery. If they do not have access to the substance, their situation is unchanged: "The others easily can possess the same materials he appropriated; the researcher's appropriation or purchase of chemicals didn't make those chemicals scarce in a way so as to violate the Lockean proviso." Nozick contends that the proviso focuses on a particular way that "appropriative actions affect others, and not on the structure of the situation that results." His concern is that people not be harmed, that their rights not be violated. But Nozick's conception of harm is narrow, focusing on harm that might be done to the property owner. Can harm be in a relative sense? That is, can people be harmed when compared to others under the same circumstances? Can we expand the concept to include the situation that results? This seems like a fair analysis because the legal structures must consider the collective good and interest. Hence, it is the relative effects resulting from the appropriation with which we must concern ourselves. To understand this in IPR, some additional information is needed.

Suppose the researcher is able to dictate the terms for the sale of the substance because the government has granted a patent. The patent provides the researcher with an advantage, specifically a monopoly advantage, in selling the product. Nozick implies that people, if they possess the right compounds, are free to make the substance. However, the patent legally blocks others from freely producing the substance themselves. Having a monopoly, the researcher is able to charge the greatest price that the market can sustain. Consequently, some will be able to afford the substance while others will not. If we use Nozick's baseline of comparison, some individuals will be made better off. They will be able to purchase the elixir, to consume it, and to rid themselves of the malady. Others will see no change in their condition because they may not be able to obtain the substance.

If the purpose of IPR is simply to protect an idea, then this has been achieved; however, nothing is said about the rights of other people to use this information except under the monopoly conditions dictated by the owner. If the purpose of the monopoly right is to make people's lives better, then one must look at the effects that this right has on all people. If the substance is available only to a segment of the population that needs it, then the remaining population is "worse-off" relative to those to whom the substance is available. So, in this sense, people in need of the substance who are unable to acquire it are "worse-off."[3] In this context, IPR cannot be justified because people have been made "worse-off" in a relative sense.

Nozick's main concern is that resources not be monopolized. Yet herein lays the contradiction between Nozick's proviso and IP: IPR promote monopolies and restrict access. Without IPR, if the researcher releases the knowledge publicly, then a contribution to the general pool of knowledge has been made. Anybody then can use the formula to produce the substance that will benefit those who need it. By restricting access to the formula as IPR do, the researcher is guaranteed a monopoly on production. The other side of this debate is that without IPR protection, the researcher would not release the information and nobody would benefit. Such an argument leads to the question of inventors' rights.

Although inventors' rights should be recognized and considered in any IPR scheme, they must be balanced with the rights of those who live with the consequences of IPR protection. In short, one must ask whether the institution of IPR is just when it provides benefits to a select few. While IPR are fair in that everybody is entitled to obtain IPR protection, the resulting product control produces distinctions among those who may need the product. This is shown clearly in Nozick's research example.

Access to advantages produced by IPR protection is thus based on financial resources, which one would expect in a competitive economy. This system is satisfactory when one is concerned about the distribution of nonessential items, that is, objects that do not affect people's physical well-being. However, IPR systems tend to treat all intellectual objects equally; they fail to recognize that not all intellectual objects are essential. For instance, people would be no worse off if they were monetarily restricted from buying a new music compact disc. But those who are monetarily restricted from buying a new drug that can save their lives are worse off than those who are not restricted. Some may contend that the social welfare net is intended to aid those who cannot afford such expenses. However, even if that is true, when an institution is expanded globally (as IPR have been), the potential inequalities are more readily exposed. Where IPR systems exist in developing nations, for example, limited resources may hinder efforts to aid those in need of product access.

In summary, Locke's labor theory of property, and its libertarian interpretation, fails to present a compelling reason to justify the existence of IPR to protect all intellectual objects. This conclusion is based on conditions present in that theory that negate the justification for property rights. Locke's labor theory does not account for the cumulative inventive process that assigns sole ownership to those who utilize others' prior work. Nozick's interpretation of Locke, based on the first Lockean proviso, insufficiently justifies IPR because people potentially are made *relatively* worse off under IPR systems, particularly as a result of unequal access to resources and products both in the domestic and global markets. Thus, one must look elsewhere in the Western tradition if IPR are to be justified under property theories. One possible approach is utilitarianism.

Utilitarians and IPR

Philosopher Will Kymlicka (1990) suggests that utilitarianism conforms to our inner sense of social responsibility; that is, the idea that the well-being of humans matters, and moral rules must be subjected to tests for their consequences on human well-being. Kymlicka argues that the morally best acts are the ones that maximize human welfare. Along these same lines, John Rawls has noted that "the principle for society is to advance as far as possible the welfare of the group, to realize to the greatest extent the comprehensive system of desire arrived at from the desires of its members" (Rawls 1971: 23-24). However, the utilitarian approach in general has come under attack from a number of scholars. The criticism is wide and varied, with the central theme being that utilitarianism does not take into account differences among individuals (Rawls 1971; Sen 1985; 1984a). As Rawls points out, "utilitarianism is not individualistic . . . in that, by conflating all systems of desires, it applies to society the principle of choice to one man" (29). Utilitarianism subjects individual rights obtained through equality and fairness to social interests. A net utility calculus formulates utilitarian social policy, which is troubling, particularly if a policy is targeted at a population segment. As Amartya Sen argues, the elimination of society's ills is justified in utility theory only if there is a net utility through their removal (1984a: 189-190). Of course, Sen's refutation has direct consequences for IPR. The burden on utilitarians is to justify property rights based on an overall improvement in the general welfare.

The utilitarians' argument is that IPR provide incentives to produce new intellectual objects. By assigning property rights to the creators, an incentive is in place for people to undertake the expense and time to invent new products or develop new ideas. If IPR are removed, the argument goes, then there will be no incentive to produce intellectual objects because people will be free to copy the object without compensating the creator. The utilitarian argument weighs the long-term development of the society against the short-term drawback of assigning exclusive production rights to a creator. Yet, it is not clear that the long-term benefits outweigh the short-term drawbacks associated with the monopoly right. These drawbacks include problems with the diffusion of technology and the varying levels of dependence that intellectual objects have on IPR protection.

The diffusion of intellectual objects is slowed dramatically under a strict IPR protection system. IP laws are meant to provide creators a time period to recover their initial investment and make a modest profit in exchange for the knowledge. As such, Edwin Hettinger sees a paradox in the utilitarian argument: the diffusion of or access to the product or method is restricted so that the production, availability, and use of new intellectual objects are assured for the future (Hettinger 1989: 48). The result is that progress is hampered.

Progress may be stalled further by the abuse of property rights that results from the buying and selling of patents, copyrights, and trademarks so that competition in the production of a commodity is eliminated. Producers then have the exclusive right to produce their product at a price that the market can sustain without competing against other products. Without competition, producers can charge artificially high monopoly prices for the product for the duration of the property right protection while being shielded from competitive pressures that force companies into product improvements.

The utilitarian justification also implies that all products and people are equally dependent upon IPR protection. Yet, this does not appear to be the case. For example, movies are more dependent on protection than academic writing, while small investors tend to rely on IPR more than large corporations (Hettinger 1989: 50). In essence, not all products or producers are equally dependent on formal IPR protection. This, however, begs the question: why do those less reliant on IPR protection keep producing? One possible answer is that the short-term profits generated by being first in the market with a product are enough incentive to engage in the productive process. As Hettinger notes, product market share is more important to large corporations than long-term IPR protection. Moreover, IP laws have been used more recently not as part of a social contract between creators and society, but as a tool for securing market share in an increasingly competitive global economy. This is especially true for producers whose intellectual objects are heavily dependent upon IPR protection.

The market share issue draws one back to the utilitarian argument that IPR provide an incentive for invention and production, which ultimately promotes economic growth. Although the incentives argument should be viewed with some skepticism, it should not be totally dismissed. Indeed, IPR can induce creative activity and production of some intellectual objects, increasing the immediate availability of products, particularly in fields that require long training or have high research costs. But this does not necessarily imply a long-term benefit of economic progress. The utilitarian argument that strong IPR protection leads to economic progress is deeply rooted in the Western theoretical tradition that emphasizes private property and its importance to Western economic development. However, the focus on private property is misplaced and such attention should instead be directed to the free exchange of ideas and creative activity that has characterized much of the West's economic growth and development.

This issue is important because it is at the core of the dispute between the industrialized countries of the North and the developing nations of the South. The North has argued that strong IPR protection will increase any country's economic progress (Gutterman 1993; Sherwood 1990; Rapp & Rozek 1990). The South generally has resisted this argument, asserting that greater access to specific technologies that aid the development process is needed. This claim has historical support. The United States explicitly prohibited the protection of foreign works for the first century of its existence. Great Britain, too, has borrowed ideas and inventions from abroad. In contemporary times, China has produced impressive levels of economic growth initially with lax IPR laws and currently with moderately strong, but poorly enforced IPR laws. Thus, it would appear that some doubt is warranted regarding the importance of strong IPR for economic progress. In essence, the utilitarian claims that the long-term benefits outweigh the short-term costs of IPR protection are weak.

The Nature of Property and Intellectual Property

Traditional justifications of property, namely labor and utilitarian, fare poorly when applied to IP. Some additional reasons for this can be seen in the distinction between traditional property and IP. Traditional property theory holds that property is not associated exclusively with individual possession. Rather, property is a relationship between the owner and other individuals relative to some item. This relationship is a right against others that can be exercised to protect the owner's property. In the case of IP, the state must guarantee the exclusive ownership of the idea or work, artificially creating the relationship between IP owners and others. For instance, in a Lockean state of nature where the power of law remains in the hands of individuals, property and IP are different. Formal law is not needed to protect that which is claimed by people; people can protect their property from encroachment by others. Intellectual property differs from simple property in this sense because there is no way to protect it. If plans for a new invention are disclosed, there is no way to prevent a person from utilizing the idea. The only way to protect IP is to keep it secret. In this way, IP is nonexclusive because it cannot prevent others from using the property once it is disclosed.

Another distinction between property and IP is supply. Using the Lockean state of nature as an example again, no one can use land that has already been appropriated. Furthermore, the supply of land is finite. Contrast this with a formula for a pharmaceutical product. Individuals can use that formula repeatedly and its supply will remain unchanged. People can pass the formula by word of mouth or by printing it and giving it away; the idea's supply will never dwindle. Moreover, the cost of an additional user of an intellectual object is zero and, as Hettinger points out, modern technology can instantaneously make an intellectual object available with few limitations (1989: 34). Without civil law, therefore, IP differs fundamentally from simple property. Society establishes laws to protect people's property from others. These laws assign rights to exclude others from using one's property. Similarly, IPR give individuals the right to exclude others from using their ideas, works, and inventions.

What IPR laws do is give the creator the ability to alter the nature of many intellectual objects by eliminating the nonexclusive characteristic. To this end, IPR grant to individuals exclusive control over some object (whether it is literary, mechanical, or procedural). IPR allow the possessor to exclude others, to control the output, and to establish a monopoly price within the limits that product demand will allow (Penrose 1951: 1-2). People who would otherwise be free to implement another's idea must now, at minimum, receive permission from and possibly pay the owner to do so. The supply of the object has thus been artificially limited by the introduction of exclusive control over distribution. As Hettinger points out, it is the non-excludable characteristic of intellectual objects that must be kept in mind when trying to justify IPR. As such, the burden on those who support strong, unlimited IPR is to show that the elimination of the nonexclusive nature of intellectual objects is justified.

The granting of exclusive control over intellectual objects is an attempt to alter their inherent structure; intellectual objects, by their nature, are nonexclusive. Traditional theories of property reflect ideas on the distribution of diminishable, perishable, or scarce property-characteristics that do not apply to intellectual objects. These objects are only made scarce by artificially imposed means, namely IPR.

In questioning the labor and utilitarian justifications for IPR, and in particular the latter account, an implicit argument is being made about the construct of IPR laws as a social policy. The focus in adopting these laws must be on the impact that an IPR system will have on individuals not society. An alternative approach that emphasizes individual needs is one possibility. However, any approach must balance the rights of creators with the needs of others.

Intellectual Property Rights Reconsidered

The utilitarian conception of IPR is centered on the benefits that society can derive by protecting IP. However, as argued above, this approach neglects the effects of these policies on individuals. The central focus of both the utilitarian arguments for society's betterment and the refutation of the utilitarian approach based on the effects of IPR on individuals, is on society's development. But these two approaches need not necessarily be treated separately. By reconceptualizing society's development at the individual level instead of at the national level, these two views can be reconciled.

Capability Theory and Economic Development

Traditionally, economic development has been explored as a country-specific phenomenon. But some have challenged this view. Development can be considered an expansion of people's capabilities (Sen 1984a, 1984b, 1985). This conception of development concentrates on individuals rather than all of society, and is carefully constructed to incorporate three often-cited definitions of development: expansion of commodities, an increase in utility and basic needs. This "capabilities approach" to economic development is an attempt to integrate all of these components while at the same time demonstrating the deficiencies of defining development solely within the context of one of these concepts.

Capability theorists define people's capabilities in terms of their functionings, which "vary from such elementary physical [needs] as being well-nourished, being adequately clothed and sheltered, avoiding preventable morbidity, and so forth, to more complex social achievements such as taking part in the life of a community, being able to appear in public without shame, and so on" (Sen 1984a: 149-50). Complex social achievements are closely linked to societal norms and will not be addressed here. For purposes of this article, the concern is with physical functionings or physical well-being, both of which may be related to societal norms, but are also subject to a series of other conditions, such as entitlement systems.

Sen has asserted that a person's capabilities depend, in part, on access to commodities, which are their entitlement. The entitlement a person has reflects the rules of the entitlement system. In this sense, IPR are a subset of the rules of the entitlement system. Yet one important proviso must be made with regard to having access to commodities that affect one's physical well-being: the emphasis is not on the actual possession of the object itself, but rather on the accessibility of the commodity. For instance, one might consider the case of a doctor patenting a medical procedure and demanding royalties for every time the procedure is used. An individual might be able to afford the operation itself, compensation for the doctor, nursing staff, hospital stay, etc., but the procedure may be made unaffordable by the additional costs of the royalties.[4] The entitlement system in this instance makes the procedure inaccessible to the individual.

The importance of access to commodities is illustrated further by two examples: music and medicine. Copyright prohibits duplication in the case of music, while patents generally protect medicines and related compounds. The music producer sets a price for the compact disc and those who can afford the music purchase it. Nobody has the right to produce that music other than the artist and the production company. Similarly, medicines are produced by a manufacturer who establishes a price for the product. Those who need to use the medicines may purchase it at that price. People do not suffer a tremendous physical loss if solely one company produces the latest music compact discs; if people cannot afford the music, they may not buy it or, alternatively, they may seek a different type of music to purchase. The free market masterfully supports substitutability of products in this instance. The medicine example is more complex and deserves greater attention.

Without much argument, medicines can be classified as important to the improvement of people's physical well-being; they are important for individuals to survive and to live better than they could otherwise. Unlike compact discs, the restricted production of particular medicines has an impact on people. Often the demand for a particular medicine is inelastic—people cannot find alternatives and they must purchase the product even if the cost escalates. If they cannot afford the manufacturer's price, they must do without the product, compromising their well-being.

Recent cases of the human immunodeficiency virus "cocktail" treatment explicitly illustrate this point. Several combinations of drugs have shown limited promise of slowing the onslaught of HIV. The drugs appear to slow the viral attack, but the cost of the drug combination is estimated at US$10,000 per year. At this price, the discovery is virtually meaningless to the many people infected with HIV around the world, particularly those in developing countries. One could easily argue that this is not an issue of IPR, but rather an issue of social welfare policy; if people cannot afford health care, it is incumbent upon the government to help them. However, this burden cannot be imposed upon governments that do not even have the economic base to feed their own people. Moreover, what this amounts to is the state subsidizing industry profits. The state is put in the bizarre circumstance of providing financial assistance to people who cannot afford medicines because the state granted the firm a monopoly on the production of the medicine.

As the music and medicine examples show, it is difficult to assume that all intellectual objects are equal in their importance to people. The existence of a hierarchy of intellectual objects is evident, but its ordering is different for each person. We cannot even assume that all individuals value the same objects as important or necessary to their physical well-being. Nonetheless, the critical point is that whatever property is needed to maintain an individual's physical well-being must be accessible if all human beings are to be permitted to achieve their full potential.

Physical Well-Being and Intellectual Property Rights

With respect to the IPR issue, developed countries have more resources available to adopt any combination of policies that will satisfy both those claiming IPR in a particular object and those who may need to use the object to maintain their physical well-being. The state, in this case, may adopt IPR protection while implementing a social welfare policy that aids those who cannot afford the product if it is needed for their physical well-being. While this may indirectly subsidize industry, it is one way for the state to balance competing interests. Developing countries, on the other hand, are restricted in the policies they can adopt because of financial constraints. If developing nations adopt IPR policies, it is possible that intellectual objects that people need will be priced outside of their ability to pay. With limited resources, the state can do little to alleviate the problem, thereby jeopardizing the physical well-being of its people.

The developing country is faced with a number of competing interests that it must balance: the needs of its people and industries, and the claims brought by foreign governments and enterprises. Foreign governments and enterprises have an interest in protecting their technological advances from duplication because every competitor producing a particular object shrinks the foreign market for the object, reducing potential profits *ceteris paribus*. People's needs have been addressed previously, leaving domestic industry and foreign entity interests for further evaluation. As argued above, inventive activity or even the process of creating some object rarely begins without reference to or building upon other work. Indigenous industrial research and technology that might help solve some of the more critical problems faced by developing nations is limited, so the least costly option is to import existing technology and to adapt it for domestic use.

While this seems to be an easy solution to the problem, the consequences of such an action are serious as this constitutes "theft." If one does not recognize intellectual objects as a form of property, then it is meaningless to discuss property rights in this regard. In such cases, the state is under no obligation to protect intellectual objects, and those with access to the product may freely copy it without fear of penalty.

Those who create intellectual objects are then left without recourse against those who profit from their work. At the other extreme is the argument that all intellectual works are property that is in need of protection from "thieves." Neither of these interpretations is satisfying.

If no IP is to be protected, individuals often will be reluctant to release their works. More importantly, this position taps into a deeper sense of fairness. If somebody toils for months on an invention and then finds it mass-produced by somebody else without compensation, that person will feel cheated. Similarly, laws that protect all intellectual objects may produce situations such as that given in the music and medicine examples. What both extremes have in common is that they evoke a certain level of moral indignation. Society is faced with two competing values: protecting those who create objects from being exploited by profiteers seeking a quick dollar on the one hand, and alleviating personal suffering of people when the capability to do so exists on the other hand. The problem is one of property rights versus subsistence rights. The approach using the physical well-being criteria provides one possible solution. In practice, nations already recognize the existence of subsistence rights through a variety of means. For example, the Universal Declaration of Human Rights recognizes such rights, while domestic social legislation in the developed countries has incorporated these basic tenets of survival (Okun 1980).

Nations may choose to adopt certain objects that are considered important to their development, but it may not be possible to justify the adoption of all intellectual objects, which leads back to the hierarchy of IP discussed above. The decision to import a particular intellectual object should be made with two goals in mind: (1) to provide for the physical well-being of the state's people, and (2) to integrate the technology into an indigenous research and development program that will contribute to solutions for some of the problems that the state faces in providing goods for the physical well-being of its people. The first of these principals, based on the hierarchy of IP, is fairly obvious in its objective. The second is intended to provide developing countries with the opportunity to break their dependency on the developed world for technology. The second provision, though important, is an ancillary goal with the immediate objective being greater access to products that will enhance people's physical well-being. Even if the developing countries adhered to these provisions for importing technology, why should any developed country and its IP creators acquiesce to such a scheme for the partial redistribution of technical knowledge? One could simply argue this position on the basis of benevolence--it helps people. But this approach neglects a glaring problem: how to balance the rights of the property creators (firms, inventors, etc.) in the developed countries with the needs of the people in developing countries.

The Duty to Bring Aid

While inventors and creators have a right not to give up their knowledge, that right may be outweighed by a duty to assist those in the developing countries. Nozick argues that rights to material things are determined by whether having the object violates the rights of another individual. Based on this argument, one might insist that the property owners in the developed countries have absolutely no obligation to provide their products to the developing countries without compensation. After all, if we consider intellectual objects to be property (as the developed countries do), they are the owners' to use as they please. Moreover, property owners in the developed countries did not create the terrible economic and social conditions that are pandemic in the developing countries; hence, IP owners have no obligation to involve themselves in solving "their" problems.[5] If developing countries want to use IP created by other countries, they must pay to do so. This position, however, is unconvincing.

John Arthur insists that in situations where people have a right not to act, there may be compelling reasons that obligate them not to exercise that right: "If it is in our power to prevent death of an innocent without sacrificing anything of substantial significance, then we ought morally to do it" (1996: 49). In such cases, the duty to help others outweighs the rights of the giver if what is being provided is of substantial significance. The problem, of course, is in how "substantial significance" is defined. Arthur asserts two criteria for determining substantial significance. First is the question of importance to the recipient:

> [W]e might specify the needs that people have, and grant that the duty to bring aid is not present unless these needs have already been met. Included among the needs which are of substantial significance would be those things without which a person cannot continue to function physically, for example,

> food, clothing, health care, housing, and sufficient training to provide these for oneself (49).

The recipient must be in need of these particular goods. Most of the points covered in this criterion relate directly to physical well-being.

The second criterion is a psychological factor on the part of the donor: "if the lack of x would not affect the long-term happiness of a person, then x is of no substantial significance." Goods or products needed to sustain happiness need not be given or sold to benefit others if the lack of the item will decrease the amount of happiness the owner could have. In other words, items that could be transferred are those considered to be of substantial significance to the people in need and of no substantial significance to the donor.

The second criterion Arthur proposes is critical because it is an attempt to balance the rights of the donor against the rights of the recipient. When applied to IPR, this principle becomes morally contentious. If one assumes that IPR provide an incentive to invent (however dubious this might be), then one must focus on the incentive as the source of happiness to the creators. Of course, there are those who invent and create things for truly altruistic reasons, but inventions and products that require high costs often have the incentive of profit returns to entice investors who ultimately own the rights to the product. According to Arthur's second criterion, if profit is what makes people happy, and by allowing their product to be duplicated they receive less profit, the producers of the IP need not allow others to copy their product because it will decrease their happiness. In cases where there is no substitution for the product, the producer has a monopoly.

The situation that Arthur's second principle creates is one of profit versus physical well-being. It is morally difficult to justify boosting profits at the expense of peoples' physical well-being. While this issue is a problem, it need not beckon the extreme Marxist position that advocates the abolition of private property. Instead, what is needed is an amendment to Arthur's second criterion with what one might call the principle of priority.

The principle of priority would recognize the property owner's right, but order this against others' rights. This assumes, as argued above, that duties can outweigh certain rights. A state must arbitrate between competing rights. In some cases, the optimal solution is a simple compromise, but in others, some rights must take priority. The question is: how would the state decide this issue? The issue is whether a person's right to pursue profits takes priority over another individual's physical well-being. (At this juncture, it is important to note that one need not be concerned, as the utilitarians are, with whether society will maximize its benefits by this decision.) Put in these terms, it is clear how the state should decide. Clearly, the state would not be able to place the right to profits over a person's physical well-being. Profits could be achieved by other means; the producers can easily find other ways of generating profit. In contrast, physical well-being is relatively limited in how it can be fulfilled. In this framework, the duplication of IP by developing countries could be considered just, given the assumption that the state would place human physical well-being morally above the right to profit.

In practical terms, the industrialized countries have an interest in seeking to improve the living conditions of the developing countries. If a goal of the developed countries is to expand their potential markets for intellectual goods, then they need viable, stable markets with healthy, educated people to purchase their technologically advanced products. It is thus in the interests of foreign entities, private and public, to assist those countries in developing sustainable economies. On the other hand, some industries see this as a potential threat because vibrant economies necessarily mean additional competition in an increasingly competitive global economy. In this view, additional competition for shrinking markets may not be welcomed, as some industries see strict IP protection as an advantage in competitive climates. However, this does not dilute the importance of the arguments already made concerning the duties to aid other developing countries. In fact, what is called into question is the position that IP is a guaranteed universal human right, the topic of the next section.

Intellectual Property and Human Rights Reconsidered

The Universal Declaration of Human Rights recognizes IP as a universal human right. However, the argument presented so far conflicts with the UN position. This article has argued that all IP is not equally significant to human well-being and that people's physical well-being must take priority in assigning IPR. This section will contend that the UN declaration is flawed and that other issues that relate to physical well-being must take priority over the guarantee of IP as a universal human right.

The United Nations and Intellectual Property

Under Article 27 of the Universal Declaration of Human Rights, IP is designated as a universal human right: "Everyone has the right to the protection of the moral and material interests resulting from any scientific, literary, or artistic production of which he is the author" (Laquer and Rubin 1989: 197-202). The basis for such a claim without doubt lies in the Western conception of property rights. What this implies is that, similar to the ownership of property, people also have an exclusive right to their ideas, creations, and inventions. In practice, the United Nations is charged with the administration of various international agreements pertaining to IP. However, its position on IP and its duty to carry out agreements promoting universal IP protection are incompatible with other important goals, particularly the promotion of human physical well-being.

The declaration of IP as a universal human right is problematic within the framework of physical well-being established in this article because the UN position does not recognize the hierarchy of IP that exists. Under the Universal Declaration, the registered trademark for a transnational corporation is accorded the same importance and protection as a patent for medicinal purposes. This position has been challenged emphatically by the developing nations with the issue again centered on the profits versus physical well-being argument. Prime Minister Indira Gandhi of India echoed these concerns when she argued that

> Affluent societies are spending vast sums of money understandably on the search for new products and processes to alleviate suffering and to prolong life. In the process, drug manufacture has become a powerful industry, subject to the same driving considerations of other big industries, that is, concentration on profit, fierce competition and recourse to hard-sell advertising. Medicines, which may be of the utmost value to poorer countries, can be bought by us only at exorbitant prices, since we are unable to have adequate independent bases of research and production. This apart,

> sometimes dangerous new drugs are tried out on populations of weaker countries although their use is prohibited within the countries of manufacture. It also happens publicity makes us victims of habits and practices which are economically wasteful or wholly contrary to good health. . . . My idea of a better ordered world is one in which medical discoveries would be free of patents and there would be no profiteering from life or death (Patel 1983: 165-166).

Article 27 may also pose problems for other rights guaranteed by the Declaration. For instance, Article 25 proclaims the universal right of every person

> to a standard of living adequate for the health and well-being of himself and of his family, including food, clothing, housing and medical care and necessary social services, and the right to security in the event of unemployment, sickness, disability, widowhood, old age or other lack of livelihood in circumstances beyond his control (Lacquer and Rubin 1989: 197-202).

The conflict with Article 25 occurs when IP protection raises barriers to commodity access that would improve the physical well-being of people. By promoting IP as a guaranteed right, the Declaration gives IP producers significant latitude in abrogating any responsibility to promote national development, though producers often argue for greater access to foreign markets and the protection of IP in those markets.

Trade, Aid, and Intellectual Property

In recent years, the West, led by the United States, has pushed for increased global protection of IP, which is in line with the UN position. Based on the previous discussion of IP protection and its relationship to physical well-being, this position could be detrimental to the developing nations. By promoting stronger protection of all IP, the developing nations will be placed at a more severe disadvantage, both in developing policies to sustain economic growth and in the increasingly competitive global markets. The result of strengthening IPR protection for developing countries may be in foregoing products that could aid in sustaining economic development, as it has been defined in this article. But more importantly for the developed countries, strong IPR protection in many of these countries will only promote continued reliance on foreign aid from the developed countries, which does little to promote economic self-sufficiency.

IP can be adapted to domestic economic conditions and utilized by the developing countries. Historically, this has been the case in a number of countries. The United States, Britain, Japan, Germany, and other developed nations have all adopted foreign inventions, creations, and ideas and adapted them to domestic use, promoting their continued growth and development. However, the developing countries are now faced with the problem of these same countries imposing greater barriers to accessing technology that could help sustain development. Strong IPR protection advocated by the developed countries is also short-sighted in that the primary concern for the developing countries is to adapt technology that will help maintain the physical well-being of their people. By putting up barriers, the developed countries delay the creation of markets that could support entry of technologically advanced IP, thus cutting short the potential profits that could be obtained if the developing countries could sustain themselves.

Conclusion

This chapter illustrates how IP is playing an increasingly more important role in the economic development of states. While the process of further technological advancement necessitates the protection of exclusive production rights that IPR grant, the maintenance and improvement of human physical well-being must be considered when allocating IPR. The resulting decision has profound human rights implications, given that the Universal Declaration of Human Rights guarantees IP as a human right. In order to maximize both the benefits derived from IP and the physical well-being of its citizens, developing and developed countries must work to craft policies that strike a fine balance between these values. Part of this work must include allowing developing countries access to critical technologies that support the economic development of their people. The trade-off for developed countries is that weaker IP protection in developing countries may ultimately result in lower foreign aid requirements as the developing world acquires technologies that allow it to sustain itself.

Chapter 2

Policy Beyond Assumptions: Intellectual Property Rights and Economic Growth*

Introduction

In part, the argument for strong IPR protection is predicated on the assumption that a positive relationship exists between strong IPR protection and economic growth and development. This chapter is dedicated to the task of providing an empirical assessment of the IPR-economic growth question. Scant empirical research has been done on this topic. One of the reasons has been the lack of consistent IPR protection data. Hence, two immediate goals unfold. The first is to provide a new measure for IPR protection. The second is to use the new measure in an empirical assessment of the relationship between IPR and economic growth.

The Measurement of Intellectual Property Rights Protection

With the increased global attention to IPR issues, scholars and policymakers have begun to focus more on IPR protection and its economic impact. One problem in conducting this research has been the measurement of IPR protection. Prior attempts seem to be limited in their ability to capture IPR protection, focusing on the laws with limited attention paid to how nations enforce those laws. The importance of the enforcement component, however, becomes even more critical given the Trade-Related Aspects of Intellectual Property Rights (TRIPS) agreement under the World Trade Organization. The TRIPS agreement requires that most nations should be in compliance with the minimum standards for IPR protection by the year 2006.[1] In practical terms the distinguishing factor among nations in the protection of IPR will be in how they enforce those laws.

The enforcement of IP laws has been a critical issue, particularly in trade relations between developed and developing countries. The measurement of such practices will be crucial in the assessment of national performance in protecting IP. This section presents an alternative method for measuring IPR protection that incorporates the strength of national IP laws and states' enforcement practices of those laws. The measure is a better gauge of IPR protection than just using the strength of laws, which may lead to greater estimation error in states' IPR protection.

The measurement of cross-national IPR protection is a critical issue for international business scholars and practitioners. For scholars, the measures can offer insightful perspectives into micro-level questions about the nature of corporate inventive activity, investment trends, research and development and corporate strategic investments. At the macro-level these data can also help address questions about the relationship between IPR and trade, foreign investment flows, and economic growth and activity. Practitioners in international business may find these data and the approach taken here valuable tools in assessing IP investment risk in countries, particularly in industries that are sensitive to the protection of IPR (e.g. pharmaceuticals and chemical industries, the entertainment and software industries, and marketing and licensing enterprises).

Empirical Research

IP has long been a concern for many industries, particularly for those with a heavy reliance on the protection afforded by national IPR laws. In many ways, as technology has advanced, industries have been victimized by their own success, because with greater advances in technology have come easier methods for duplicating that same technology and associated products. For instance, the introduction of video recorders to consumer markets also brought with it the capacity to duplicate videotapes, bringing about potentially massive violations of entertainment industry copyright protection. As such, advances in technology have made some industries more reliant than other industries on IP protection. The pharmaceutical and chemical industries are highly dependent on patent protection (Nogues 1990; Noonan 1990; Sherwood 1990; Comanor 1986; Besen and Raskind 1991) as a consequent of technology that has reduced the difficulties in duplicating chemical compounds. Other industries such as the entertainment industry and computer software industry have reliance on copyrights and patents for the same reasons (Band and Katoh 1995; Ebanks 1989; United States Congress 1986; Besen and Raskind 1991). Much of this research, however, has been qualitative, with few quantitative studies. One obstacle to doing quantitative IPR research has been in constructing measures of IPR protection. A number of studies have attempted to measure IPR protection cross-nationally; among them are Rapp & Rozek (1990), Seyoum (1996) and Sherwood (1997).

Rapp and Rozek's study was one of the first attempts to quantify IPR protection in some form. Scholars used this measure in their studies (Gould and Gruben 1995), and the US government cited this study as providing additional evidence to support its position on global IPR (Wichterman 1991). Hence, Rapp and Rozek's measure warrants closer scrutiny. They use patent laws as a proxy for IPR protection. They measured the strength of 159 countries' patent laws on a zero to five scale, where zero represents a country with no patent laws and five represents a country that has laws consistent with the minimum standards established by the US Chamber of Commerce Intellectual Property Task Force (Rapp and Rozek 1990a 7; 1990b 79; Gadbaw & Gwynn, 1988 11, 51-55). The Rapp and Rozek 0-5 measure is presented in Table 2:1.

Table 2:1 Rapp and Rozek's Patent Protection Scale.

Score	Description
0	No intellectual property protection laws
1	Inadequate protection laws; no law prohibiting piracy
2	Seriously flawed laws
3	Flaws in laws, some enforcement laws
4	Generally good laws
5	Protection and enforcement laws consistent with minimum standards proposed by the US Chamber of Commerce

Source: Rapp & Rozek, 1990 Appendix 4.

Seyoum (1996) also used the US Chamber of Commerce's minimum standards for his criteria. However, his 0-3 scales of IPR protection components were constructed from surveys sent to IPR practitioners. After validating the responses against each other and against existing literature, Seyoum constructed four variables (patents, copyrights, trademarks and trade secrets) for use in his analysis.

Sherwood (1997) proposed a third measure of IPR protection that combined personal knowledge and experience with professional interviews. The protection scores theoretically range from 0-103 and were developed for eighteen countries. Eight major components comprised Sherwood's measure summarized in Table 2:2 (Sherwood, 1997: 265). The conditions for rating countries were derived from the US Chamber of Commerce Guidelines, but the relative weights were derived mostly from the author's experience (Sherwood: 265-267). Similarly, the points assigned under any category to a country were also based on the author's experience (Sherwood: 267). Interviews with local attorneys augmented the author's experience, particularly with the enforceability component.

Table 2:2 Sherwood's Intellectual Property Rights Components

Description	Assigned Points	
Enforceability	25	
Administration	10	
Substantive Law		
Copyright		12
Patents		17
Trademarks		9
Trade Secrets		15
Life Forms		6
Treaties	6	
Total	100	
Public Commitment	3	
Total Possible Points Added	3	

Source: Sherwood 1997: 265.

Each major component contained sub-categories for which each country could lose points based on observed deficiencies in the total points allocated for that major component. For instance, the enforceability component (worth 25 points in the coding scheme) contains eight separate areas of interest to the author: judicial independence (up to 12 points), quality of judges (up to 10 points), lack of legal tools for enforcement (up to 10 points), judicial knowledge of IP concepts (up to 7 points), reliability of prosecutors, police, and customs officials (up to 6 points), civil and criminal sanctions (up to 6 points), delays in enforcement proceedings (up to 4 points), and the lack of transparency for final decisions (up to 2 points). Deficiencies in these components resulted in the subtraction of points ranging from a high of 12 for judicial independence to a low of up to 2 points for the final transparency issue. The amount to be subtracted was again based on interviews and the author's experience.

The sub-category point deductions were then subtracted from each component total score. All component scores were then added to obtain the aggregate IPR measure for each country. Finally, an impressionistic assessment of the public's commitment to IP accounted for up to three additional points, which were then added to the eight major components. This final step made the theoretical total points for each country 103. In practice the final scores ranged from high of 83 for the Bahamas to a low of 13 for Guatemala.

Research Assessment

While each study makes important contributions in assessing the strength of IPR protection in countries, several conceptual and measurement issues are raised. The first conceptual issue is which IPR laws must be examined to gauge protection. Rapp and Rozek's measure assumes patent laws *ipso facto* represent all IPR laws. However, services increasingly are accounting for larger portions of economic growth. The value of a name or identification therefore has significant economic impact. Particularly in Western countries, the economic contributions of copyrighted software production, entertainment products, and publishing are significant. To discount these two forms of IP protection would be to underestimate their economic impact. Similarly, it has been argued elsewhere (Ostergard 1999; Hettinger 1989) that states do not treat all IP equally. Some forms of IP are more important to nations' economies than others. Using patents as a proxy for all IPR may overlook this issue. While Seyoum assesses the strength of these laws individually, Sherwood's measure blends five different forms of IPR laws into the score. The combining of various laws into one conceptual measure of IPR protection may present some theoretical and methodological difficulty.

A second conceptual issue relates to the enforcement of the laws. Rapp and Rozek and Seyoum do not include a component for enforcement in their study, though Rapp and Rozek recognize the issue (1990a: 7). The logic behind this proposition is intuitively simple. States may have in place the institutional structures and financial resources to enforce these laws, but others that do not have these structures and resources may not be able to enforce the laws adequately. Sherwood too recognizes this issue by including an enforceability component in his measure, but it does not significantly address the behavior of the governing regime in enforcing the IP laws. The enforcement component Sherwood uses reflects an assessment of the *potential* to enforce IPR laws and not an assessment of the regime's *actual* performance.

From a measurement perspective, all three researchers assign scores based on the laws in force at the time they coded their data. Changes and amendments to the laws that may have occurred during any specific time period are not taken into account. The temporal element becomes critical particularly when using such measures to gauge the effect of IPR on foreign direct investment, technology levels and industry and economic growth. The missing temporal element means that their measure will not capture the impact of changes to these laws.

Another measurement concern is the replicability of these measures. For instance, Rapp and Rozek do not explain what constitutes the difference between a score of two and a score of three. What is the difference between "inadequate" laws and "seriously flawed" laws or the difference between "generally good laws" and laws that are "fully consistent" with the minimum standards? Without clearer criteria, an element of subjectivity is introduced, which casts doubt on the measurement's validity and reproducibility. In Seyoum's study, it is unclear as to how the raw data were reduced to a 0-3 scale. Similarly, because Sherwood's study is based preponderantly on the author's expertise, the ability to replicate the results without that vast experience is limited. Moreover, because the procedures use on-site interviews in the country, the practicality of duplicating these measures across time and across countries is limited as well.

A second concern with Sherwood's procedures is that because they are largely based on his experience, they may be more subjective than is desirable. For instance, when judging how many points to subtract for judicial independence, no set rules exist for what does constitute judicial independence. What criteria are used to subtract 5 points versus 6 points? We cannot be certain about distinctions given that the assessment is grounded in personal perception. Moreover, there seems to be some incongruity between the total points assigned to the major components and the total points that can be subtracted in the sub-categories. For instance, the enforceability component itself is worth 25 points, but the sub-category points that can be subtracted total 57 points. Is it possible that countries could have a negative score for enforceability? In theory, it is a possible scenario.

The Concept of Intellectual Property Rights Protection[2]

The measurement of IPR must incorporate both a statute component and an enforcement component. Roughly categorized, nations' laws can range from having no laws to having the strongest laws, and enforcement practices can range from having no enforcement of the laws to having strong enforcement of the laws. As Sherwood (1997) also notes, a nation can have strong laws or weak laws, but unless those laws are enforced, they are virtually non-existent in terms of the protection afforded IP owners and investors.

Law Measurement

To measure the strength of IPR laws, two issues must be addressed: what IPR laws and by what standards? I have settled for using just patents, copyrights and trademarks because the bulk of IP is protected under these laws (Benko 1987) and the information on cross-national patent, copyright, and trademark laws is more readily available than for other types of IP laws. Following the practice of the other three studies, this study is based on the minimum criteria for IPR laws established by the US Chamber of Commerce. Using these criteria, separate code sheets for patent, copyright and trademark laws were created to conduct a content analysis of countries' IP laws[3]. A number of legal sources were used to complete code sheets for each country in this study. All sources used pertained to IP statutes only, without reference to prior judicial review, trial histories or customs. The laws for seventy-six nations were coded twice with different coders utilizing the same code sheets.[4] A comparison of the two codings showed inter-coder agreement to be high; all inter-coder agreement scores were .90 or higher. This score reflects a 90 per cent or higher agreement between coders on all items coded, which also indicates that these code sheets were constructed such that coding replication could be reasonably achieved. The laws for each nation were coded for three time intervals, 1988, 1991 and 1994. Three year intervals were used because the laws were not expected to change much on an annual basis. The time period was chosen because of the temporal limits of the enforcement component.

Enforcement Measurement

The enforcement score of the IPR protection measure was obtained through content analysis as well. Under the 1988 Omnibus Trade and Competitiveness Act, the United States Department of State was mandated legislatively to track the status of the IP laws and enforcement practices of the United States' trading partners. These assessments appear in the US State Department's book, *Country Reports on Economic and Trade Practices.* These reports are produced semi-annually and began in 1989. Hence, the data set is temporally limited to the post-1988 period. The early reports do not distinguish among the different types of IPR laws as the later reports do. The enforcement code sheet, which contains only one variable, was constructed to gauge a general assessment of the enforcement of IPR laws in the country.[5] Coding of the enforcement practices was done for 1988, 1991 and 1994 (whereas the reports began in early 1989, it was assumed information gathered was for 1988 and reported in 1989). The laws for each year were coded twice by separate coders using the same code sheet with inter-coder reliability scores all over .90.

Scale scores of the IPR laws were obtained using Guttman scaling procedures (Garson 1976; MacRae 1970; McIver and Carmines 1981). Any polychotomous items were converted to dichotomous variables. A gamma matrix, measuring the strength of association among all variables, revealed that not all the variables clustered together (with a gamma score of .80 or higher) to form one scale of IPR laws. In fact, the clustering that did occur was within each individual type of law. This finding has *theoretical significance* in that it confirms the idea that states *do* treat these laws differently and that there is no unidimensional concept of IPR law. Each type of law *must* be treated distinctly from others.

The variables were then ordered and summated according to Guttman scaling procedures (Garson 1976; MacRae 1970; McIver and Carmines 1981). This procedure produced three scales: patents (0-5), copyrights (0-10) and trademarks (0-8). In these scales, zero represents no laws while the other ends of the scales represent the strongest laws. Tests of reproducibility and scalability were conducted on the scales. Coefficients of reproducibility were above .90 and all coefficients of scalability were above .60, the minimum acceptable levels for Guttman scaling.

To obtain complete IPR protection scores for each nation and each type of law, the scale score for each nation and law was multiplied by the enforcement score for each nation, which ranged from zero to four. Zero represents no enforcement of IPR laws while four represents the strongest enforcement. The multiplication of these two measures signifies that the law *and* the enforcement component are both *necessary conditions*. Because enforcement information could not be obtained for each type of law for each year, it is assumed that the enforcement practices apply to all the laws. In later years, the State Department reports assessed the enforcement of type of law, making individual enforcement scores for each type of law feasible in future studies.

The multiplication of the enforcement and law components is not problem-free. First, it creates great variation in the data from country to country. For instance, the multiplication of a country's patent score of 3 with its enforcement score of 3 creates a score of 9. The same procedure for a country with a patent score of 3 and an enforcement score of 1 creates a score of 3. Is the relationship between the enforcement and the law component multiplicative or additive? And by inference what weights should be given to the enforcement component? Two ways of dealing with both questions exist; the first is grounded in the assumptions of the research question, the second is methodological.

In multiplying the two scores together, the underlying assumption is that the laws and the enforcement are *necessary* conditions for IP *protection*. Laws must be enforced in order to provide substantive protection. Researchers, however, may be inclined to believe that the enforcement is not a necessary and separate policy issue from the enactment of the laws, rather that enforcement is simply another component of protection and is weighted no differently than the laws. The researcher may even find that the laws themselves have a deterrent effect and that the correct approach is to consider the scores to be additive. However, the issue is one of formulating the research assumptions. The benefit of these data is that both assumptions can be accommodated. Because the laws and the enforcement components are separate entities, the researcher is free to make the assumptions deemed appropriate. Should the researcher assume a multiplicative relationship, then some additional work is needed to address the question of how to weigh the enforcement component in the multiplicative relationship.

By taking the log of each of the variables, the data distances are reduced and the researcher can utilize the data in linear-log or log-log models. Moreover, the weights for each of the components are adjusted automatically by virtue of the log function.[5] Both model types are quite common in business, economics and political science studies where data are often characterized by wide variations cross-sectionally or temporally.

Reliability and stability coefficients for the IPR protection scores were calculated across the three panel waves (Heise 1971). The coefficients show that the measures are reliable across the three-wave panel design, with all reliability coefficients at .98 and higher. However, the stability of these measures varies. The stability of the copyright variable is high across all time periods (.879, .950, .830). Patents are stable over the first two waves (.993), but the stability decreases over the second and third waves (.769) and from the first to the third waves (.764). Trademarks reflect the greatest decline in stability over the three waves. While highly stable over the first and second waves (.984), the stability coefficients show a large decline over the second and third waves (.595) and from the first to the third waves (.588). This finding would indicate that trademarks have undergone the most change over the six year period.

IPR Protection Score Analysis

Correlations between the IPR protection scores and Rapp and Rozek's patent scale scores, Sherwood's IPR scores and Seyoum's three new IPR measures were calculated for the countries in the IPR protection data set; these results are presented in Table 2:3. The matrix shows that Rapp and Rozek's scale scores correlate inconsistently across the three types of IP laws and protection. The highest correlations are with patent laws and protection, which correlate at .56 and higher. The lowest correlations were with trademark laws and copyright protection. While patents are moderately correlated with Rapp and Rozek, the other two forms of IPR protection do not correlate highly. The copyright and trademark variables' low correlation with Rapp and Rozek's patent variable is further indication of the theoretical importance of treating IP law components separately. One measure can not be used as a proxy for the other because nations do not assign equal importance and attention to them.

Table 2:3 IPR Protection Measures Correlations, 1988-1994

Variable	Rapp & Rozek (N=76)	Sherwood (N=18)	Seyoum (N=23)
1988			
Copyright	**.51	.28	*.42
Patent	**.66	.19	**.65
Trademark	**.50	.13	**.61
1991			
Copyright	**.56	.41	*.47
Patent	**.71	.24	*.47
Trademark	**.60	.34	.32
1994			
Copyright	**.43	.30	*.50
Patent	**.57	.13	*.56
Trademark	**.45	.16	*.51
Rapp & Rozek	1.00	.31	
Sherwood	.31	1.00	
Seyoum Patents	**.88	.004 (N=7)	
Seyoum Trademark	**.60	-.23 (N=7)	
Seyoum Copyright	**.57	.10 (N=7)	

* p <.05, **p<.01

Seyoum's measures reflected moderate positive correlation with the IPR protection scores, with the highest correlations in the area of patent protection and the lowest correlations in trademark protection. There was no significant correlation between any IPR protection scores and Sherwood's measures, which is most likely due to the low number of observations available in Sherwood's data set.

The correlations among the other variables were also mixed. The strongest correlations were between Seyoum's patent measure and Rapp and Rozek's measure (.883), indicating a close relationship between the two. There was moderate correlation between Seyoum's measures for trademarks and copyrights and Rapp and Rozek's patent measure. Sherwood's measure had a low level of correlation with Rapp and Rozek's measure. However, the low and insignificant correlations of Sherwood's measure with Seyoum's measure cannot be assigned much importance given the low number of cases the two data sets had in common.

Additionally, the low correlations among the IPR protection scores and the other scores may be a product of the differences in the methodology used to create these data. The enforcement component in the IPR protection score has the capacity to enhance or to detract from the strength of the laws. It is possible that nations may have weak laws but strong enforcement of those laws or strong laws but weak enforcement of them. Measures that do not capture this distinction will correlate modestly with measures that do.

The Debate: Intellectual Property Rights and Economic Growth

One study empirically tested the relationship between IPR and economic growth. Gould and Gruben (1996) found that stronger IPR protection corresponds to higher economic growth rates across countries (345), though these effects may be tempered in less competitive, closed markets. Their findings lend support to the developed countries' claims of significant economic benefits to be derived from increasing patent protection.

Gould and Gruben begin with a benchmark model for comparative purposes. The purpose of this model is to gauge the effects of IPR on economic growth once major economic factors are considered. Their dependent variable is the log of the average annual per capita gross domestic product (GDP) between 1960 and 1988.[6] The independent variables include: the log of GDP in 1960, the log of gross domestic investment as a share of GDP, and literacy rates in 1960, which measures the stock of human capital. In an addition to the model, the log of government consumption and dummy variables for assassinations, revolutions and coups, and for geographic location in Latin America and Africa are added. Assassinations and revolutions and coups are proxy variables for political stability. No theoretical justification is given for the geographic indicator variables. Gould and Gruben then add the IPR variable, which is Rapp and Rozek's patent protection measure, to the model.

Using OLS regression, they find no significant relationship between IPR and economic growth. They then proceed to apply an instrumental variable approach to the analysis, which assumes that the IPR variable is a proxy for other variables. This procedure is tantamount to two-stage least squares analysis. Based on their assumption, instrumental variables were used to predict the IPR scores. The predicted scores were then used in the model. The results showed that IPR have a marginally significant ($p<.10$) effect on economic growth. This finding is supported in qualitative research prior to Gould and Gruben.

Most often, the work of Joseph Schumpeter is cited in support of IPR protection. Schumpeter's work focused on the idea that innovation and technology are *the* driving forces in industrial development. Hence, the protection of IPR becomes even more crucial if one falls into the Schumpeterian school of thought. Those supporting IPR argue that strong protection provides several benefits (Gutterman 1993: 120):

Increased domestic research and development
Increased flow of new products
Enhanced value of patent rights
Increased inward investment and technology transfer
Improvements in the local knowledge base

What makes these five points noteworthy is that they are most often characteristic of advanced, industrialized countries that do not face the specific issues that developing countries confront. Most developing countries do not have the capacity for domestic research and development, giving developed countries a decided advantage in the production of new products and processes. Even if developing countries want and can afford the new products, often the question of whether the product is appropriate arises. For example, does a country such as Mali, an extremely underdeveloped country, need to import laptop computers when the resources could be better used feeding its people? This example is extreme but serves to illustrate the point.

The third point, the increased value of patent rights, is least important to developing countries and one of the most important to developed countries. In industrially developed countries, the patent (and other IPR forms such as copyrights and trademarks) is the source of monetary value for ideas and is the guarantee that others cannot legally copy the idea. It is also the basis for the incentives argument that proponents of strong IPR make. Incentives are needed to induce people to produce particular objects beneficial to society. Again, this point is well taken, but it has more application to developed countries than to developing countries that may be trying to acquire *existing* technologies and processes to help in their development processes.

What are most important to developing countries are investment, technology transfer and local knowledge building. With these issues comes a complex myriad of social and economic problems associated with them. While investment and technology transfers are seen as goals to strive for, they can act as a double-edged sword in that they also increase expectations and change attitudes in developing countries. Of the potential problems, the influence of developed country social and economic standards on developing country salary scales, elite lifestyles, and wealth accumulation provide a basis for caution in seeking investment and technology transfer (Todaro 1994: 53). Moreover, when such investment and technology transfer does occur, there is no basis to believe that local knowledge may be increased. In fact, transnational corporations may be reluctant to allow certain types of technology to be adopted for fear of losing their competitive advantage in these markets. Hence, the promise of increasing local knowledge bases often is hollow. Given these associated issues, there is reason to exercise caution in accepting the *prima facie* arguments of improved economic benefits for developing countries if they adopt strong IPR.

The Economic Model

To gauge the effect that IPR protection has on economic growth, a benchmark or base model of economic growth must be established. Following Gould and Gruben (1996) the base model with four variables that provide measures of consumption, investment, and labor capacity is established. These variables include government consumption, investment as a percentage of GDP, population, and the physical quality of life index (PQLI). Population is used to control for the size of the country while the PQLI is used as a measure of human capital. In addition to these variables, GDP_{t-1} is used to account for the assumptions made by the partial adjustment model used in the estimation.

The Partial Adjustment Model

The partial adjustment model assumes that nations have a target or a preferred level of GDP in a given year (t). It also accounts for the idea that nations may be able to attain only a fraction ($1-\alpha$; where $0<\alpha<1$) of what they want toward their target on average each year. GDP is a function of the previous period's level of GDP plus an adjustment toward their target, which can be represented by the following equation:

$$\text{Log}(GDP_t) = (1-\alpha)\,\text{Log}(GDP_{t-1}) + \alpha\,(\text{Log}(GDP_t))$$

The coefficient $1-\alpha$ is an adjustment coefficient since it indicates the rate of adjustment of GDP_{t-1} to GDP_t. After one period, $1-\alpha$ of the gap between GDP_{t-1} and GDP_t is closed so that α of the gap remains. After N periods, the gap closed will be $1-\alpha^N$ (Kamenta 1986: 530). Thus, it can be written that $1-\alpha^N=p$ and the number of periods to close the gap can be written as

$$N = \frac{\log(1-p)}{\log(p)}$$

By including GDP lagged in the equation, we can estimate both the short-term and the long-term effects of IPR protection on GDP across countries. With this, the base model can be written as

$$GDP_t = f(GDP_{t-1}, \text{Government Consumption}, \text{Investment/GDP}, \text{Population}, \text{PQLI})$$

This model is used to analyze data for two periods, 1995 and 1991. Data for IPR protection could not be obtained prior to 1988, so estimation of its effects on GDP in 1988 could not be obtained. The first two models are for GDP 1995 regressed on variables at times t-1 and t-2 while the third model represents GDP 1992 regressed on variables at time t-1.

The variables used in the model represent standard economic factors used in the analysis of economic growth. Gould and Gruben chose government consumption as a proxy for government spending in the economy. As the government demands more goods and services in the economy through expenditures, the output of the economy can be expected to increase. Investment in GDP serves as a proxy for the amount of physical capital savings in the economy or how much capital is present in the economy. Gould and Gruben use literacy rates to approximate human capital; however I have substituted this for the PQLI, which includes literacy rates and other factors affecting human capacity or potential (Morris 1979). All these variables are expected to have a positive effect on GDP, both in the short term and long term.

Base model results

The results of the base model are presented in Tables 2:4-2:6. They show that population, PQLI and GDP in the prior periods are generally significant, though PQLI drops out of significance in the third equation. Surprisingly, consumption and investment, standards in econometric models of GDP, are insignificant. This finding may be the result of the short time period used in these analyses. GDP is typically analyzed using time-series data. However, these models are limited temporally due to the lack of available data. The interpretation of the coefficients in the partial adjustment model does not differ from that of ordinary least squares regression (OLS) except for the inclusion of the long-term parameter estimates. In the long term, each coefficient is divided by the adjustment coefficient (1-α) where α represents the coefficient of the lag GDP variable. For example if we use the coefficients from the first equation results, a one per cent increase in population in 1991 leads to a .115 per cent increase of GDP in the short term and in the long term a one per cent increase in population leads to a 1.359 per cent (.115/(1-.914)) increase in GDP.

Table 2:4 Model Results Dependent Variable GDP 1995

Variable	Short Term Estimate		Long Term Estimate
	Coefficient	t-stat	Coefficient
Intercept	-0.42	-1.22	-4.99
Ln(GDP 89)	0.91	***33.31	10.75
Ln (Cons 88)	0.12	1.45	1.39
Ln (Inv/GDP 88)	0.03	0.40	0.35
Ln (Pop 88)	0.16	***3.69	1.35
PQLI 1988	0.004	**2.83	0.058

Adj R^2 =.99; n=72 * p<.05; ** p<.01; *** p<.001

Table 2:5 Model Results, Dependent Variable GDP 1995

Variable	Short Term Estimate		Long Term Estimate
	Coefficient	t-stat	Coefficient
Intercept	-0.16	-0.95	-3.19
Ln(GDP 92)	0.95	***59.94	18.71
Ln (Cons 91)	0.037	0.70	0.73
Ln (Inv/GDP91)	0.034	0.67	0.67
Ln (Pop 91)	0.063	***3.74	1.24
PQLI 1988	0.003	***3.36	0.06

Adj R^2 =.99; n=72 * p<.05; ** p<.01; *** p<.001

Table 2:6 Model Results, Dependent Variable GDP 1992

Variable	Short Term Estimate		Long Term Estimate
	Coefficient	t-stat	Coefficient
Intercept	-0.28	-1.121	-6.59
Ln(GDP 89)	0.95	***47.22	21.99
Ln (Cons 88)	0.09	1.50	2.08
Ln(Inv/GDP 88)	0.009	0.17	0.21
Ln (Pop 88)	0.06	**2.62	1.39
PQLI 1988	0.002	1.60	0.04

Adj R^2 =.99; n=72 * p<.05; ** p<.01; *** p<.001

With the base model established, the variables of particular interest, the IPR protection variables, may be added to gauge their effect. These results are presented in Tables 2:7-2:9. The results including the IPR protection variables are inconsistent. While the base model variables remain consistent, with population, PQLI, and GDP_{t-1} being significant, the significance of the IPR variables is inconsistent. However, the slope values and directions are consistent over the three periods. Most surprising are the negative slopes on the patent and trademark variables. In substantive terms, for GDP 1995, a one point increase in patent protection in 1988 would lead to a .013 per cent decrease in GDP in the short-term and a .17 per cent decrease in the long run. A one-point increase in trademark protection would lead to a .011 per cent decrease in GDP in the short-term and a .141 per cent decrease in the long-term. Copyright protection has a positive slope and in the short term, for each point increase in copyright protection, a .009 per cent increase in GDP would result. In the long term, that point increase would yield a .12 per cent increase in GDP. These results are inconsistent for the second 1995 analysis, but consistent with the 1992 analysis. One possible reason for this discrepancy may be the severe economic recession in the Western economies, which may be reflected in the 1991-1992 data.

Table 2:7 IPR Model Results, Dependent Variable GDP 1995

Variable	Short Term Estimate		Long Term Estimate
	Coefficient	t-stat	Coefficient
Intercept	-0.67	*-1.90	-8.77
Ln(GDP 89)	0.92	***34.62	11.99
Ln(Cons 88)	0.16	*1.96	2.13
Ln(Inv/GDP 88)	0.02	0.31	.30
Ln(Pop 88)	0.11	***3.75	1.45
PQLI 1988	0.006	**3.47	.07
Patent 88	-0.01	-1.48	-0.17
Copyright 88	0.009	**2.67	0.12
Trademark 88	-0.01	**-2.44	-0.14

Adj R^2=.99; n=72 * p<.05; ** p<.01; *** p<.001

The results also show significant features regarding IPR protection. First, when compared to other economic factors, the effects that IPR have cross-nationally are relatively small, with IPR protection contributing marginally to GDP. Second, should a nation adopt a policy of full, strong protection across the three types of IPR, the net impact is estimated to be negligible or negative given the direction of the patent and trademark coefficients. While these results apply to all

Table 2:8 IPR Model Results, Dependent Variable GDP 1995

Variable	Short Term Estimate		Long Term Estimate
	Coefficient	t-stat	Coefficient
Intercept	-0.31	-1.54	-7.77
Ln(GDP 92)	0.96	***49.89	24.03
Ln (Cons 91)	0.07	1.32	1.86
Ln (Inv/GDP 91)	0.01	0.18	0.25
Ln (Pop 91)	0.05	***3.06	1.39
PQLI 1991	0.003	***3.36	0.08
Patents 91	-0.008	-1.61	-0.18
Copyright 91	0.003	1.16	0.07
Trademark 91	-0.003	-0.70	-0.06

Adj R^2=.99; n=72 * $p<.05$; ** $p<.01$; *** $p<.001$

Table 2:9 IPR Model Results, Dependent Variable GDP 1992

Variable	Short Term Estimate		Long Term Estimate
	Coefficient	t-stat	Coefficient
Intercept	-0.38	-1.47	-10.17
Ln(GDP 89)	0.96	**49.30	25.54
Ln (Cons 88)	0.10	*1.69	2.75
Ln (Inv/GDP 88)	0.008	0.14	0.21
Ln (Pop 88)	0.05	***2.60	1.51
PQLI 88	0.003	*2.07	0.06
Patents 88	-0.004	-0.592	-0.10
Copyright 88	0.006	**2.522	0.17
Trademark 88	-0.01	***3.16	-0.27

Adj R^2=.99; n=72 * $p<.05$; ** $p<.01$; *** $p<.001$

countries in the dataset, the question that still needs to be addressed is: do these results vary for developed and developing countries? As noted earlier, one primary assumption being made in this research is that developed and developing countries have different objectives, which mean they will emphasize policies differently. Additionally, as discussed previously, the benefits of strong IPR protection may be different for developed countries than they are for developing countries. Thus, it would be beneficial to look at these groups of countries separately.

Developed and Developing Countries

To compare the impact that IPR protection has on economic growth, I follow the same procedure established in the previous chapter. The data set is split on the mean PQLI score in 1988. Countries above the mean are scored a one and those below the mean are scored zero. The partial adjustment model equation was then run for each sub-group. The base model results presented in Tables 2:10-2:12.

Table 2:10 Model Results, Dependent Variable GDP 1995, Developed Countries

Variable	Short Term Estimate		Long Term Estimate
	Coefficient	t-stat	Coefficient
Intercept	-0.74	0.95	-11.71
Ln(GDP 89)	0.93	***18.50	14.68
Ln (Cons 88)	0.26	1.57	4.139
Ln (Inv/GDP88)	-0.003	0.02	-0.05
Ln (Pop 88)	0.09	1.41	1.49
PQLI 1988	0.002	0.31	0.04

Adj R^2=.99; n=33 * p<.05; ** p<.01; *** p<.001

Table 2:11 Base Model Results, Dependent Variable GDP 1995, Developed Countries

Variable	Short Term Estimate		Long Term Estimate
	Coefficient	t-stat	Coefficient
Intercept	0.19	0.45	170.34
Ln(GDP 92)	0.99	***37.57	893.45
Ln (Cons 91)	-0.03	-0.38	-27.67
Ln (Inv/GDP91)	0.07	1.05	71.54
Ln (Pop 91)	0.005	0.19	5.35
PQLI 1988	-0.003	-0.58	-3.00

Adj R^2=.99; n=33 * p<.05; ** p<.01; *** p<.001

Table 2:12 Model Results, Dependent Variable GDP 1992, Developed Countries

Variable	Short Term Estimate		Long Term Estimate
	Coefficient	t-stat	Coefficient
Intercept	-1.06	-1.74	-17.27
Ln(GDP 89)	0.93	***23.81	15.24
Ln (Cons 88)	0.27	*2.08	4.40
Ln (Inv/GDP88)	-0.05	-0.48	-0.87
Ln (Pop 88)	0.08	*1.68	1.43
PQLI 1988	0.006	1.07	0.11

Adj R^2=.99; n=33 * p<.05; ** p<.01; *** p<.001

The results for the developed countries are consistent, though the population and PQLI variables drop in significance. This finding is not surprising given that there is much less variance in these variables as a result of sub setting the data. The results from the second equation in Table 2.11 appear to be unusual. A clear indication of this is the lagged GDP variable. The coefficient is .998, which indicates the close correspondence between GDP 1995 and GDP 1992. Compare this with the GDP 1992 and GDP 1988 coefficient, which is .93. This coefficient shows less of a correspondence with GDP 1992 than GDP 1992 has with GDP 1995. Hence, the recession in developed economies during the early 1990s is illustrated clearly, with little growth in the 1992-1995 period. The interpretation of the coefficients is the same as in the previous section in both the short term and the long term. The one surprise in these results is the negative coefficient on the investment and consumption variables. These run counter to expectations, but may be a function of the cross-national design of the test. The next step is to add the IPR protection variables. The results for these are presented in Tables 2:13-2:15.

The directions of the copyright and trademark coefficients are consistent across the three tests. However, only the trademark coefficient in the last equation is significant. Consistent with the results from the full dataset, the IPR variables appear to have a negligible affect on GDP with these variables in both the short term and the long term contributing much less than 1 per cent to GDP. The same procedures are followed for those below the mean 1988 PQLI.

Table 2:13 IPR Model Results, Dependent Variable GDP 1995, Developed Countries

Variable	Short Term Estimate		Long Term Estimate
	Coefficient	t-stat	Coefficient
Intercept	-1.01	-1.37	-16.73
Ln(GDP 89)	0.93	19.56	15.40
Ln (Cons 88)	0.30	*1.94	5.01
Ln (Inv/GDP88)	-0.02	-0.18	-0.39
Ln (Pop 88)	0.11	*1.83	1.88
PQLI 1988	0.002	0.33	0.04
Patents 88	0.003	-0.35	0.06
Copyright 88	0.004	1.08	0.08
Trademark 88	-0.01	**-2.56	-0.23

Adj R^2=.99; n=33 * p<.05; ** p<.01; *** p<.001

Table 2:14 IPR Model Results, Dependent Variable GDP 1995, Developed Countries

Variable	Short Term Estimate		Long Term Estimate
	Coefficient	t-stat	Coefficient
Intercept	-0.02	-0.06	-27.37
Ln(GDP 92)	0.99	***29.12	989.09
Ln (Cons 91)	0.01	0.14	13.08
Ln (Inv/GDP91)	0.06	0.78	63.02
Ln (Pop 91)	0.01	0.29	10.54
PQLI 1991	-0.002	-0.39	-2.33
Patents 91	-0.005	-0.81	-5.05
Copyright 91	0.004	1.26	4.07
Trademark 91	-0.004	-0.97	-4.62

Adj R^2=.99; n=33 ** p<.001

Table 2:15 IPR Model Results, Dependent Variable GDP 1992, Developed Countries

Variable	Short Term Estimate		Long Term Estimate
	Coefficient	t-stat	Coefficient
Intercept	-1.14	*-2.07	-21.07
Ln(GDP 89)	0.94	***26.73	17.49
Ln (Cons 88)	0.28	**2.42	5.18
Ln (Inv/GDP88)	-0.06	-0.65	-1.14
Ln (Pop 88)	0.09	*2.12	1.80
PQLI 1988	0.005	1.01	0.10
Patents 88	0.003	0.43	0.06
Copyright 88	0.002	0.62	0.03
Trademark 88	-0.01	***-3.24	-0.24

Adj R^2 =.99; n=33 * p<.05; ** p<.01; *** p<.001

The results (Tables 2:16-2:17) show a closer resemblance to the full dataset's results than did the results for the developed countries. PQLI and the population variables remain significant in the first two models, though they drop out of significance in the third.

Table 2:16 Base Model Results, Dependent Variable GDP 1995, Developing Countries

Variable	Short Term Estimate		Long Term Estimate
	Coefficient	t-stat	Coefficient
Intercept	-0.58	-1.00	-9.080
Ln(GDP 89)	0.93	***20.52	14.61
Ln (Cons 88)	0.06	0.73	1.05
Ln (Inv/GDP88)	0.02	0.23	0.34
Ln (Pop 88)	0.09	*2.28	1.48
PQLI 1988	0.006	***3.20	0.10

Adj R^2 =.99; n=38 * p<.05; ** p<.01; *** p<.001

Table 2:17 Base Model Results, Dependent Variable GDP 1995, Developing Countries

Variable	Short Term Estimate		Long Term Estimate
	Coefficient	t-stat	Coefficient
Intercept	-0.26	-0.91	-4.10
Ln(GDP 92)	0.93	***29.29	14.30
Ln (Cons 91)	0.05	0.74	0.85
Ln (Inv/GDP91)	0.04	0.57	0.68
Ln (Pop 91)	0.07	**2.79	1.19
PQLI 1988	0.005	***4.04	0.08

Adj R^2 =.99; n=38 * p<.05; ** p<.01; *** p<.001

Table 2:18 Base Model Results, Dependent Variable GDP 1992, Developing Countries

Variable	Short Term Estimate		Long Term Estimate
	Coefficient	t-stat	Coefficient
Intercept	-0.13	-0.36	-3.89
Ln(GDP 89)	0.96	***29.57	27.58
Ln (Cons 88)	0.02	0.44	0.83
Ln (Inv/GDP88)	0.01	0.20	0.38
Ln (Pop 88)	0.04	1.60	1.35
PQLI 1988	0.002	1.61	0.07

Adj R^2 =.99; n=38 * p<.05; ** p<.01; *** p<.001

Again, we add the IPR variables to the model. These results are presented in Tables 2:19-2:21. The results show again no consistent pattern illustrating significant effects of IPR protection on economic growth. What little consistency there is comes from the patent protection variable. The negative direction of this variable holds across all three models, but its significance does not. The patent variable is significant only in the second 1995 GDP model.

Table 2:19 IPR Model Results, Dependent Variable GDP 1995, Developing Countries

Variable	Short Term Estimate		Long Term Estimate
	Coefficient	t-stat	Coefficient
Intercept	-0.76	-1.36	-11.07
Ln(GDP 89)	0.93	***18.61	13.55
Ln (Cons 88)	0.09	0.82	1.35
Ln (Inv/GDP88)	0.07	0.73	1.12
Ln (Pop 88)	0.10	**2.21	1.45
PQLI 1988	0.007	***3.07	0.10
Patents 88	-0.007	-0.62	-0.10
Copyright 88	0.007	1.11	0.11
Trademark 88	-0.001	-0.16	-0.02

Adj R^2=.99; n=33 * $p<.05$; ** $p<.01$; *** $p<.001$

Table 2:20 PR Model Results, Dependent Variable GDP 1995, Developing Countries

Variable	Short Term Estimate		Long Term Estimate
	Coefficient	t-stat	Coefficient
Intercept	-0.60	*-1.73	-14.15
Ln(GDP 92)	0.95	***26.15	22.52
Ln (Cons 91)	0.12	1.57	2.93
Ln (Inv/GDP91)	-0.04	-0.53	-1.07
Ln (Pop 91)	0.07	**2.51	1.68
PQLI 1991	0.005	***3.72	0.12
Patents 91	-0.15	*-1.89	-3.71
Copyright 91	-0.007	-1.29	-0.17
Trademark 91	0.01	*1.82	0.34

Adj R^2=.99; n=33 * $p<.05$; ** $p<.01$; *** $p<.001$

Table 2:21 IPR Model Results, Dependent Variable GDP 1992, Developing Countries

Variable	Short Term Estimation		Long Term Estimation
	Coefficient	t-stat	Coefficient
Intercept	-0.33	-0.85	-9.32
Ln(GDP 89)	0.96	**27.56	26.94
Ln (Cons 88)	0.04	0.58	1.27
Ln (Inv/GDP88)	0.06	0.91	1.88
Ln (Pop 88)	0.04	1.52	1.34
PQLI 1988	0.002	1.57	0.07
Patents 88	-0.007	-0.58	-0.21
Copyright 88	0.008	*1.81	0.24
Trademark 88	-0.006	-0.96	-0.17

Adj R^2=.99; n=33 * p<.05; ** p<.01; *** p<.001

Discussion

Earlier studies have suggested that IPR have a positive effect in a number of ways in promoting economic growth and that these benefits are universal in nature. The underlying assumption of this research is that all countries behave similarly and have similar goals that would motivate them to adopt a strong IPR regime. This assumption, however, is misleading. Even prior empirical work done on this topic found only marginal benefits to be gained from strong IPR protection.

Using a different measure of IPR protection, no consistent evidence emerged to show that IPR contributed significantly to economic growth cross-nationally. Furthermore, when the nations are split into developed and developing countries, results to suggest otherwise did not emerge. More important are the negative coefficients attached to many of the IPR variables. The negative coefficient implies that states may see negligible effects and quite possibly negative effects from adopting strong IPR protection, though the significance of these effects is low.

One possible reason for the weak findings in this chapter is that the temporal range of the study is limited. A time series dataset may have produced stronger results. It may be possible that IPR protection takes a long time to work through the economic system of a country, limiting our ability to show any short-term impact. Also, time series analyses of individual countries over a longer period would provide better comparisons amongst different types of countries in terms of how IPR protection affects developed and developing countries.

Despite the drawbacks with the analysis, the findings give researchers and policymakers some evidence to exercise caution regarding the assumed relationship between IPR and economic growth. In fact, the analyses raise additional research questions to be explored, particularly regarding the role of IPR in promoting economic growth in developing countries. For instance, the coefficient for patent protection in developing countries is consistently negative and larger than the same coefficient for developed countries. This finding suggests that the impact of patent protection varies by a country's development. The obvious question that emerges then is: what motivates a developing country to adopt strong IPR protection, particularly if it may be harmful?

Chapter Three

What is best for the rest?: The Political and Economic Determinants of Intellectual Property Rights Protection

Introduction

The IPR debate between the developed and developing countries emerged in its most contentious form in the 1980s as nations began moving from protectionist policies to free-trade and free-market oriented economies. The developed countries collectively sought to pry open large, untapped consumer markets in the developing world. But as trade with and investment in developing countries increased, developed countries expressed strong dissatisfaction with the fairness of the domestic markets in these countries, particularly with regard to the treatment of foreign products. Specifically, corporate leaders voiced concern over the lack of protection their products were afforded in foreign markets from pirating and imitation. They contended that foreign piracy of their IP had cost them billions of dollars and had eliminated millions of jobs in their home countries. Ideas had become the new economic battleground between developed and developing countries. When IPR became a central trade issue, a number of states modified or completely overhauled their IPR systems. However, given the findings presented in the last chapter, a state's decision to adjust IPR protection is not necessarily voluntary, but may be a product of internal and external conditions. States are faced with domestic pressure to strengthen or to enforce existing IPR laws, pressure from foreign governments demanding strong protection for the IP of their TNCs or a combination of both. The goal of this chapter is to examine both the domestic and international factors that affect a state's IPR policy. Two questions are to be addressed: (1) which factors both domestically and internationally affect states' IPR protection policies and (2) do these factors differ for developed and developing countries? The evidence presented here suggests that both domestic and international factors have a role in determining a state's IPR policies and that these factors do differ for developed and developing countries.

Empirical Research

Empirical research on the determinants of IPR protection is scarce. The lack of research may be due to a combination of several factors. First, there has been little interest in IPR outside of the legal profession. The subject has been addressed tangentially by economists, even though innovation and invention are recognized as major components of economic growth and development (Kuznets 1972; Malecki 1991). Political scientists have recently begun to address the issue as a point of economic and political conflict among states. In short, this is a relatively new field of inquiry for social scientists. Second, as addressed in the previous chapter, the measurement of cross-national and cross-temporal IPR protection has been a daunting task for researchers and scholars. Finally, there has been an underlying assumption, particularly in the legal profession, that the protection of IPR by all countries is good for all actors involved. States with weak IPR protection are "outlaw" nations that are uncooperative in promoting economic growth and investment. Hence, there was little need for empirical research on IPR protection. However, given historical and contemporary examples (detailed in the remaining chapters), the last point should be approached with some skepticism.

Rapp and Rozek (1990) addressed factors that affected how states protect IP. Using regression analysis, they found that the level of economic development correlates closely with the level of patent protection (1990: 7). Rapp and Rozek interpret this finding as clear evidence of the need for strong IPR protection to promote economic development. In this study, patent protection is used as a proxy measure of IP protection. As noted previously, the measure they use is inadequate given the nature of IPR, which cannot be viewed as a unidimensional concept to be measured by patent laws only.

Moreover, Rapp and Rozek do not present the results of their regression analysis. No regression coefficients or standard errors are presented with their findings. Despite these issues, the importance of the Rapp and Rozek study can not be overlooked. They present one of the first attempts to measure IPR protection and to explore the relationships associated with it. Though they do not present the empirical results, their study is the first to proclaim an empirical relationship between economic development and IPR protection. Additional research on this question is thus warranted.

To understand the factors that contribute to a state's IPR protection policies, we must be concerned with the sources of pressure that come to bear on governments. These pressures emanate from both the domestic and international levels. At the domestic level, industries that have an interest in protecting their IP exert pressure on governments to enhance IPR protection. These industries tend to be high technology industries or industries that are on the cutting-edge of technology and whose products are susceptible to IP piracy or whose product life is short due to rapidly changing technology. In the US, for example, the chemical and pharmaceuticals industry, the computer industry, and the motion picture industry have been most vocal in pressing the government to increase protection at home and abroad (see chapter four for details about these industries).

At the international level, states that are the recipient of large amounts of trade and investment come under pressure from foreign governments, particularly of developed countries, to increase IPR protection. The most watched example of this in recent years has unfolded in China. The opening of China's domestic market to foreign investment has proven to be an economic boom to investors and a major problem for IP owners. Corporations whose investments and trade are dependent on strong IPR protection protested vehemently to their home governments about the lack of adequate protection for IP in China. Under the threat of trade wars with the United States, the Chinese government increased the protection afforded IP under its laws and stepped up enforcement of existing laws. Cases where foreign pressure has been applied to increase IPR protection are not limited to China. Developed countries, led by the United States, pressured Taiwan, South Korea, Japan, Thailand, Philippines and numerous other countries to change their IPR protection practices.

The Empirical Model

The empirical model to be tested here is on the assumption that states do not voluntarily adopt strong IPR protection, particularly at earlier levels of development. The most relevant factors are sources of either domestic or foreign pressure on the existing regime. For this model, technology and democracy represent factors at the domestic level while global integration and foreign direct investment represent international level factors. From these, four specific hypotheses about IPR protection can be tested.

H_1: The more technologically advanced a state is, the stronger will be its IPR protection.

H_2: The more democratic a nation is, the stronger will be its IPR protection.

H_3: The more globally integrated a nation is, the stronger will be its IPR protection.

H_4: The more foreign investment a state receives, the stronger will be its IPR protection

Theoretically, states that have higher levels of technology should want to protect the investments their citizens make in IP products. Those states with lower levels of technological development would be better off "stealing" innovations. The costs of implementing patents and licensing agreements may prove too expensive to implement. Thus, even at low levels of technological development, some nations may be better off having weak IPR protection in order to stimulate the adoption of technologically sophisticated products (Lall 1976: 12; Gutterman 1993: 122). States therefore strategically adopt IPR policies based on their technological needs. Additionally, states with higher levels of technology should experience greater pressure to implement and enforce strong IPR regimes, particularly from those industries that are IPR-dependent, such as the chemical and entertain-ment industries.

Additionally, the political nature of the regime should have a positive impact on the IPR protection a state will accommodate. This relationship is based on two factors. First, democratic governments generally recognize and attempt to protect property rights of any kind. Government respect for property rights historically has been a critical issue in the relationship between governments and their citizens. Second, democratic governments, by their nature, are open to greater influences from pressure groups that are dependent upon IPR protection for their goods.

At the international level, two relationships are postulated. The more states are integrated into the global economy, the more likely they are to protect IPR. Integration in this case is defined as how much a country trades. If states do not adequately protect IP, foreign governments may intervene on behalf of their transnational corporations to pressure target states to strengthen IPR protection. IPR protection has also been cast in terms of trade issues because corporations exporting IP to states with weak IPR protection lose export market share to those companies that freely pirate IP products in a target country. On the one hand, the more a state trades, the more likely it will be exposed to pressure to increase its IPR protection. On the other hand, it is also possible that the more a state trades, the less likely it will be to protect IPR. This argument has to do with the protection of domestic industry. If a country has strong IPR protection, this creates an artificial monopoly in that country for any product. If the protection is for a foreign product, then domestic producers will be legally blocked from entering markets to produce these products. States therefore may want to delay, either by legislation or in practice, strong IPR. By not having weak laws or not enforcing laws states create a non-tariff barrier to entry in domestic markets for foreign producers. Foreign producers can not compete with the lower production costs of pirates who duplicate IP from foreign sources. Therefore, there is an incentive to keep IPR protection weak to enhance domestic industry production.

Similarly, calls to increase IPR protection come from those that invest in states. Investors who are willing to invest money in a country to produce goods will want strong IP protection so that their investments will be guaranteed. If they lose money due to IPR infringement, they may seek assistance from their home governments in pressuring the target country to increase IPR protection. Theoretically, the more a country receives in foreign investment, the greater the pressure will be from foreign sources to protect IPR.

Data and Measurement

The data set for this study is the IPR dataset developed in the previous chapter. Variables for technology, democracy, foreign investment and integration have been added based upon the procedures described below.

Technology Levels

The measurement of technology levels is a complicated and controversial process. Aggregate science and technology indicators have been addressed by a number of scholars across several disciplines. Each procedure has both positive and negative aspects. Three measures of note have been looked at for this study: bibliographic indicators, domestic patents issued by a country, and technology component measures. Frame (1984) discussed the use of bibliographic information (the number of scientific articles published in a country) as an indicator of a country's level of scientific achievement. This measure is appropriate for addressing questions that deal with the structure of a country's research system, research trends, scientific dependency on outsiders, or scientific communication patterns in some countries (121). However, its use as an aggregate indicator of scientific achievement is questionable because research may be hidden by several factors including the inability to write in English, time sensitive research where there is no time to publish results, lack of clerical support, and disinterest in local country problems (120). Hence, these numbers may seriously under-represent scientific activity in a country.

Another measure of science and technology used by Frame (1987) is the number of domestic patents issued by a country. Frame argued that this measure is a good indicator of a country's technological capacity. However, the use of this measure in this study would present obvious methodological problems. These data are also misleading because they do not distinguish the type of technology patented. A child's toy is treated equally as a pharmaceutical product. While these data may measure inventive capacity, it seems doubtful that they are able to measure with any confidence technological capacity.

What both these measures lack is a conceptual foundation for what exactly comprises technology and how to measure those components. Reynolds and Krivo (1996) address this idea when they called attention to Frisbie and Clarke's work on comparative technology measures.

Frisbie and Clarke conceptualize technology as having six distinct components, which are shown in Table 3:1.

Table 3:1 Frisbie and Clarke's Technology Measurement Model

Component	Indicator
Energy Use	1. Consumption of coal, lignite, petroleum, natural gas, hydroelectric and nuclear energy
Agriculture	2. Tractors in use 3. Fertilizer consumed
Manufacturing	4. Cement produced 5. Steel consumed in industry 6. Tin consumed in industry
Transportation	7. Aviation (km flown) 8. Railway freight (ton-km) 9. International sea-borne shipping (metric tons) 10. Motor vehicles in use, passenger and commercial
Communication	11. Radios in use 12. Telephones in use 13. Televisions in use 14. Newsprint consumed 15. Domestic telegrams 16. Domestic mail 17. Total daily circulation of newspapers
Information	18. Scientists, technicians, and engineers 19. R&D expenditures per scientist and engineer 20. R&D expenditures as a percentage of GNP

Source: Reynolds and Krivo (1996).

Each component measures a particular type of technology. As Reynolds and Krivol discussed, each component in no way is a complete indicator of leading technology. Collectively, they tap into a society's basic capacity for subsistence, productive, supportive and informational technology cross-nationally and temporally (Reynolds and Krivo 1996: 102-103).

In replicating Frisbie and Clarke's measure, Reynolds and Krivo transformed the data. Each indicator was divided by population and then the natural log was taken for these measures. The measures were then converted to z-scores relative to the mean and standard deviation of each indicator for the entire time period. According to Frisbie and Clarke, this was done to achieve a constant scale across the various indicators of technology (105). A score for each component of technology was then calculated as the mean of the z-scores for a component indicator. They collapsed the component indicators to five by combining the transportation and communication components. Scores for all the components were then added to achieve a single index and then adjusted to a scale of 0-100, with 0 representing the lowest technology and 100 the highest. This procedure was used in a data set comprising 98 countries from 1950-1990 with data every ten years for each country.

Conceptually, this index has appeal. It attempts to include major facets of what intuitively is a country's base technological capacity. The major drawback to this measure is the availability of data. While these data are available for the 1950-1990 time periods (every ten years), they were not available for the time period of this study, 1988-1994 (the chosen time period of this study will be discussed in detail later). Developing countries in particular are not able to report these data frequently due to resource and data collection problems. Even in Reynolds and Krivo's study, the information technology component could only be included for dates prior to 1990. Therefore, in attempting to replicate this measure, a number of changes had to be made due to the availability of data.

Variables that indicated any measure of the consumption of a particular commodity were changed to production variables. This change allowed for easier gathering of some data. More importantly, the change reflects a stronger interest in being able to tap into a nation's productive capacity. Because of data availability problems, some variables could not be obtained. Of the eighteen variables used, complete and uniform data could be obtained for eleven of them. These variables are listed below in Table 3:2.

Table 3:2 Technology Index Variables

Component	Indicator
Energy Use	1. Total production of Energy (TPES), which includes all of Frisbie and Clarke's energy indicators
Agriculture	2. Tractors in use
Manufacturing	3. Cement produced 4. Tin produced
Transportation	5. Railway freight (ton-km) 6. International sea-borne shipping (metric tons) 7. Motor vehicles in use, passenger and commercial
Communication	8. Radios in use 9. Telephones in use 10. Televisions in use 11. Total daily circulation of newspapers

Data for the information technology variables were not available consistently across countries and times for 1988-1996. Following Reynolds and Krivo, all variables were divided by population.

Instead of transforming these data as Reynolds and Krivo did, I chose to factor analyze these data separately for each of the three years in this study. This procedure is not a major departure from Reynolds and Krivo, as they report that various transformations of their data all yield highly correlated indices of technology. Among the transformations they attempted was to obtain factor scores by factor analysis, which correlated at .95 or higher with the procedure they decided to use. Factor scores were then derived for each country. Correlation analysis among all three years showed the reliability and stability of the new technology measures (Heise 1971). Tables 3:3 -3:4 present these data.

Table 3:3 Correlation Matrix for Technology Index

	Technology 1988	Technology 1991	Technology 1994
Technology 1988	1		
Technology 1991	.994	1	
Technology 1994	.983	.991	1

Table 3:4 Reliability and Stability Coefficients for Technology Index

	Coefficient
Reliability	1.00
Stability $_{88\text{-}91}$	.991
Stability $_{91\text{-}94}$	.988
Stability $_{88\text{-}94}$	.980

All the technology variables correlate highly. The reliability coefficient of 1.0 indicates that the measures are internally consistent. The stability scores for each combination of years indicated that the measures are stable across time. The high stability coefficients are theoretically consistent because we would not expect much fluctuation in a state's technological capacity over a short period of time.

Global Integration

The term global integration, or globalization, connotes several different definitions incorporating both political and economic concepts. Globalization, as it has been termed by some, has been the subject of much literature that tries to define it in some precise manner. This task seems to be dependent upon the research question at hand. For the purposes of this study, I am particularly interested in a country's relationship to the global economy. I adopt Van Bergeijk and Mensink's definition of globalization or global integration as the basis of a network of nations that links economies through various financial transactions, particularly trade, foreign direct investment, and labor migration (1997: 159).

Most developed countries are major exporting countries whereas developing countries tend to be import dependent. Relative to the concept of integration into the global economy, this may create discrepancies in the importance of exports to one set of countries (developed countries) and the importance of imports to another set of countries (developing countries). One way of thinking about this is that without those countries importing, exporting countries would have fewer markets. By using exports only, the importance of the importing country is marginalized. Also, by using exports as a proportion of GDP, the measure is capturing the significance of exports to the domestic economy, but it really says little about how much exposure the country has in the global economy. The argument that is being made here is that the more exposure a country has at the international level, the more likely it will be to have stronger IPR protection. By using total trade, the importance of both import and export-dominant countries is taken into account. To weigh a country's relative importance in the global economy, the total trade figure is then taken as a proportion of world total trade. The exposure that a country has to the global economy is recognized without prejudice to the type of exposure, be it exports or imports.

Democracy

To measure the level of democracy in states, I have adopted Ted Robert Gurr's (1996) democracy scale. This variable, often used in international relations literature and empirical modeling, measures a state's level of democracy on a zero-to-eleven additive scale, with a zero representing absolutely no democracy in the country and eleven representing a democratic government. Gurr and Jaggers (1995) operationalize democracy based on three criteria: (1) the competitiveness and openness of executive recruitment, (2) the competitiveness of political participation and (3) the level of constraints placed on the chief executive. Other aspects of democracy, such as the rule of law, checks and balances, and civil rights are treated as means to or manifestations of the three institutional criteria. Their theoretical conceptualization of democracy is thus broken down into five separate dimensions and appropriate scores for each dimensional component (see Gurr 1996 and Gurr and Jaggers 1995 for these dimensions). The scores are then added to obtain the democracy scores for each country.

Foreign Direct Investment

Foreign direct investment is measured by a country's net capital inflow investment from overseas. These data are taken as a proportion of the nation's GDP in order to control for the size of the economy. For instance, a two billion dollar inflow of investment into Guatemala would have a greater impact on its economy than a two billion dollar inflow of investment into Germany's economy.

Model Results

Two initial methodological problems had to be addressed. First, using the PQLI in the model to evaluate differences between developed and developing countries was problematic because of the PQLI variable's high correlation with the technology variable, which created problems of multicollinearity (the two variables correlated at .72). This presents a problem if we are to understand what factors contribute to a state's IPR protection level. Instead of utilizing the PQLI variable, I split the data using the mean of the technology variable. Second, because the dependent variable IPR protection contains ordinal level data, OLS regression analysis is inappropriate (Liao 1994; Eliason 1993; Lewis-Beck 1980; Kleinbaum 1994; King 1989). Instead, ordered logistic regression was used to test the models. The results of the analysis for developed countries are presented in Tables 3:5-3:7.

Table 3:5 Ordered Logit Model for IPR Protection, Patents 1988-1994, Developed Countries

Variable	Estimate	Standard Error
Integration	12.38	8.71
Democracy	0.02	0.08
Technology	2.26	***0.43
Foreign Investment	2.07	0.06
n=77 Log-Likelihood=298.85 $\chi^2(4)$=46.86 Prob.>χ^2=.000 Pseudo $R^{2=}$.46		

***p<.01

Table 3:6 Ordered Logit Model for IPR Protection, Trademarks 1988-1994, Developed Countries

Variable	Estimate	Standard Error
Integration	-3.19	8.73
Democracy	0.23	***0.09
Technology	2.45	***0.44
Foreign Investment	2.18	8.20
n=77 Log-Likelihood=288.85 $\chi^2(4)$=53.53 Prob.>χ^2=.000 Pseudo R^2=.50		

***p<.01

Table 3:7 Ordered Logit Model for IPR Protection, Copyrights 1988-1994, Developed Countries

Variable	Estimate	Standard Error
Integration	12.06	8.90
Democracy	0.34	***0.10
Technology	2.08	***0.42
Foreign Investment	1.92	8.23
n=77 Log-Likelihood=322.36 $\chi^2(4)$=53.35 Prob.>χ^2=.000 Pseudo R^2=.51		

***p<.01

The results for the three types of IPR protection measures are generally consistent. The two variables that represent domestic sources of pressure, democracy and technology, are all positive factors in determining the probability of a state's IPR protection level. Though democracy is not significant for patent protection, the technology variable remains a key factor in all three model results. For developed countries, the push for stronger IPR protection, according to the results, emanates from domestic forces. Does this condition hold for developing countries? Tables 3:8-3:10 present results for these countries.

Table 3:8 Ordered Logit Model for IPR Protection, Patents 1988-1994, Developing Countries

Variable	Estimate	Standard Error
Integration	56.09	**24.67
Democracy	-0.04	0.04
Technology	-.12	0.58
Foreign Investment	-3.23	7.74
n=129 Log-Likelihood=522.07 $\chi^2(4)$=8.31 Prob.> χ^2=.08 Pseudo $R^{2=}$.06		

**p<.05

Table 3:9 Ordered Logit Model for IPR Protection, Trademarks 1988-1994, Developing Countries

Variable	Estimate	Standard Error
Integration	47.76	**24.04
Democracy	-0.06	0.04
Technology	0.62	0.58
Foreign Investment	12.70	7.74
n=129 Log-Likelihood=572.90 $\chi^2(4)$=9.821 Prob.> χ^2=.04 Pseudo R^2=.07		

**p<.05

Table 3:10 Ordered Logit Model for IPR Protection, Copyrights 1988-1994, Developing Countries

Variable	Estimate	Standard Error
Integration	55.62	**24.12
Democracy	-0.01	0.04
Technology	0.15	0.58
Foreign Investment	17.28	**7.77
n=129 Log-Likelihood=637.21 $\chi^2(4)=10.95$ Prob.> χ^2=.02 Pseudo R^2=.08		

**p<.05

The results for the developing countries have several interesting aspects when compared to those for the developed countries. First, the overall model for the developing countries tends to be a weaker predictor of IPR protection levels than the model for the developed countries. Both the log-likelihood estimate and the pseudo-R^2 are weaker for the developing countries than for the developed countries. Second, the factors that are consistent across the three model results are the sources of pressure for increased levels of IPR protection. For all the models, foreign sources (integration and foreign investment) are the significant variables in predicting IPR protection levels for developed countries. In all three models, the integration variable is significant while the foreign investment variable is significant only for copyright protection. What these results clearly illustrate is that the more developing countries are exposed to international trade and investment, the greater will be the pressure on those states to increase the level of protection for IP. Domestic factors, democracy and technology, had not significant role in any of the models for the developing countries.

Discussion and Conclusion

When combined with the empirical analysis presented in chapter two, the results predicting the level of IP protection for developing countries take on a distinct importance. We expect states to act rationally in deciding what type of protection to afford IPR. They must balance competing factors in devising policy in this area that is suited to their needs at that moment in time. What the analysis in chapter two illustrated was that there were no clear domestic economic benefits for developing countries to maintain strong IPR protection. The economic growth benefit has been the primary argument that developed countries use in trying to persuade developing countries to adopt strong protection measures. Clearly, that argument is, at best, on shaky ground. If this is the case, why would developing countries adopt stronger IP regimes? The answer to this comes from the analysis presented in this chapter.

Developing states have no incentive to adopt strong IPR protection measures on their own. It is rational for these states to obtain IP as inexpensively as possible. As I noted in chapter one, there is historical precedent for this rationale. Modern developed countries often undertook policies that would be considered "piracy" by today's standards. In practice, the rationale is a proven method for advancing technological and economic development, tested frequently and successfully by many of today's developed countries during their history. Developing countries that have weak IP protection are doing nothing more than following historically proven methods for advancing development. This proposition, however, is too simple and does not convey the dynamics at work in the IPR problems between developed and developing countries.

While the methods for acquiring IP may not have changed much, with piracy being a centuries-old practice, the *environment* in which piracy occurs has changed. In the information age the nature of industry and time have manipulated the environment in which states and other actors operate. Entire industries are sometimes dependent upon strong IP protection to maintain a competitive edge in international markets. IP protection creates monopoly market conditions that industries utilize for greater profits. However, these conditions also have been compromised with the advancement of technology that can rapidly disseminate information across the globe. The rapid spread of information compromises market exclusivity for industry producers. On the one hand, these conditions alone appear to promote developed countries' arguments for strong IP protection. On the other, the need for strong IP protection must be placed into an appropriate context.

Developed countries' calls for strong protection are advanced in the name of protecting overseas markets for their industries. These countries are acting to protect a major source of economic growth—foreign trade—for domestic industries. The irony is that developed countries have promoted policies that are intended to encourage developing countries to open their domestic markets to foreign competition. The logic behind free trade policies is that every state engaged in trade will benefit. When developing countries have opened their markets, developed countries have applied strong political and economic pressure for developing countries to protect foreign IPR. These pressures have produced the odd scenario of developing countries financing and promoting the economic growth of developed countries, possibly to the detriment of their own economic growth and development. This represents *the development dilemma* faced by developing countries: if they open their domestic markets to trade, they face political and economic pressure to protect foreign IP; if they protect foreign IP, they create conditions that force them to abandon their goal to obtain IP as inexpensively as possible. This problem is highlighted in the case studies of the United States, China and South Africa that follow.

Chapter Four

United States Trade-Related Intellectual Property Rights Policy in a Changing Global Environment

Introduction

By the end of the 1960s, most observers realized that the United States (US) was undergoing dramatic change in its position within the global economy. Countries that had been devastated economically during World War II by this time had recovered and were ready to challenge the US in international markets. But the US reaction to the rise of new competitors was plagued with problems. American industry scrambled for protection against the new competition while US lawmakers were quick to lay blame for the rising competition on unfair foreign trade practices. This combination of industrial parochial interests and lawmakers looking outward for someone to blame for the US economic "decline" created the domestic conditions that brought about the new concerns for the protection of IPR.

This new wave of concern is centered on the globalization of industry. Industries expand beyond their home borders when domestic markets become saturated and pressure to increase profits builds. When IPR-dependent industries expand internationally, they seek protection for their IP in markets to which they plan to export. Typically these new markets are in developing countries that are undergoing economic expansion. It is these markets where demand is highest for new products. For example, it is more reasonable to export goods and services to South Korea, an emerging and industrializing country, than it is to Laos, an impoverished Asian country with a minimal industrial base. To compete with the onslaught of imports coming into their countries, industries in these emerging markets obtain technology as inexpensively and as efficiently as possible.

The globalization of US industry and the emergence of IPR-dependent industries are the subjects of this chapter. Set within the context of the general background on the evolution of US trade policy, two primary arguments emerge. First, American lawmakers overreacted to the US "decline," providing industry leaders with an environment that would promote protectionist policies in the face of increasing global competition. Second, industrial influence in the IPR issue is examined. By assessing globalization and foreign market conditions that affected three particular industries, the pharmaceutical and chemical industry, the computer and software industry, and the entertainment industry, a clear relationship between competition and profit-loss appears. These conditions drove interest groups to request intervention by the US government in the foreign IPR issue on both a bilateral and a multilateral basis.

The Early Experience with Intellectual Property Rights

The American government's commitment to strong IPR has been a major component of US foreign economic policy. In 1988, The US Congress passed legislation the mandated higher tariffs for states that, in the judgment of the US Trade Representative, do not adequately protect US IP abroad. However, the US position is only a relatively recent phenomena; the US was not always concerned with global protection of IPR.

In 1787, the Founding Fathers wrote into the Constitution Article I Sect. 8, which established the powers of the US Congress. "The Congress shall have the power...to Promote the progress of Science and useful Arts, by securing for limited times to Authors and Inventors the exclusive Right to their respective writings and discoveries." By itself, Article I. Sect.8 amounts only to a recommendation to implement a copyright and patent protection system. However, by the end of 1790, the Congress took the initiative to protect IP with the passage of the first copyright law of the US. The new law provided protection for written works. But most interesting was the exclusion of foreign works from protection:

> ...[N]othing in this act shall be construed to extend to prohibit the importation or vending, reprinting or publishing within the United States, of any map, chart, book or books, written or printed, or published by any person not a citizen of the United States, in foreign parts or places without the jurisdiction of the United States (US Congress OTA, 215).

England, from which the United States adopted its initial IPR laws, was the only European country that had implemented a system of IPR protection. This fact contributed to doubting the wisdom of the IP system. For example, Thomas Jefferson, a prolific inventor in his own right, noted in 1813:

> It is a fact, as far as I am informed, that England was, until we copied her, the only country on earth which ever by general law, gave a legal right to the exclusive use of an idea. In some countries it is something done, in a great case, and by a special and personal act, but generally speaking, other nations have thought that these monopolies produce more embarrassment than advantage to society; and it may be observed that the nations which refuse monopolies of invention are as fruitful as England in new and useful devices (US Congress OTA, 216).

The exclusion of foreign works in both copyrights and patents allowed the US to obtain technology for mass distribution early in its development. In fact, the policy was encouraged by leaders such as George Washington, who had advocated "the introduction of new and useful inventions from abroad" and "the exertions of skill and genius in producing them at home" (Cohen 1995: 243). The introduction of European technology into the US without proper compensation continued for more than one hundred years, despite revisions to laws of the United States in 1802 and 1823 (Bugbee 1967: 115). The period of the highest technology acquisition under these conditions was from 1790 to 1850.

One important example of this technology acquisition came with the emergence of American railroad technology during the period

1825-1840. More than a dozen American engineers had visited England with the purpose of acquiring the knowledge and the skills to build railroads in the US.

> As a result, the American engineers developed knowledge of railroads in three areas: (1) locomotives and inclined planes, the two "new" elements in railroads, (2) the uses of materials especially stone wood and iron in construction, and (3) the principles of laying out routes feasible for railroad travel...Many of the early railroads built by the visitors were imitations of the most impressive British railroads, the Liverpool and Manchester...The visiting engineers transferred virtually an entire technological "package" to the United States (Stapleton 1978: 65-66)

The transfer of this technology was one of the clearest and best documented examples of what would be termed IP piracy by today's standards. The people who transferred the technology are well documented and the procedures they used are well known. Moreover, the railroads were distinctly new during the period; they were not an American product (Stapleton 1978: 69).

It is no historical accident that during the early stages of development, the US advocated and practiced the theft of IP from foreign sources in much the same manner the US claims developing countries are doing in the modern era. As the US developed economically, patent and copyright laws became more stringent, ultimately protecting foreign inventors who registered their works in the US.

The US "Decline" and International Competition

The post-World War II period marked a new era in American history. The US reluctantly took the international leadership role that it had shunned after World War I. In areas such as defense, international finance and trade, the US led the way in creating the post-war world order that would govern the international system even to the present day. While the US was the premier military power, the US also emerged as the dominant economic power in the post-war period. With the economies of Western Europe, Eastern Europe, and Asia devastated by the war, the US moved into the role of economic superpower in the international system, though this position would not last. American dominance in high technology sectors and other economic areas raised concern with the European allies and others. By the 1960s, European concerns emerged over the long-term consequences of US technological dominance. These concerns would quickly dissipate, however, as the technological gap between the US and its European allies closed through the 1960s. It is this period that some scholars pinpoint as the beginning of US hegemonic decline (Kindleberger 1981; Nelson 1990; Nelson and Wright 1992) and the start of economic convergence among the Western powers (Abramovitz 1986).[1] While it is unclear that there has been a global economic convergence, the evidence suggests that there was a technological convergence among the industrialized countries (Nelson 1990).

Signs of economic convergence appeared in Japan, West Germany, France and Great Britain through increases in real GDP per employed person (Nelson 1990). Additionally, these countries experienced increases in the trade of technology-intensive products, though the US maintained its edge in this area. Japan, however, made significant gains by capturing 24.5 per cent of the OECD export market in technology-intensive products by 1990 (Table 4:1). In 1959 US firms

Table 4:1 Export Market Share in Technology-Intensive Products

Country	1970	1980	1990
United States	28.3	24.1	25.6
Japan	12	16.8	24.5
West Germany	16	15.6	12.9
France	7	7.7	6.9
United Kingdom	9.5	10.8	8.3

Source: Organization for Economic Cooperation and Development, *OECD Science and Technology Indicators* (Paris: OECD, 1986) in Nelson (1990: 12).

held 79 per cent of the world market in high technology producing industries, but in 1978, they held only 47 per cent (Smith 1990). The US faced substantial technological competition beginning in the 1960s with the re-emergence of the post-war economies of Europe and Japan. But why was it possible for these economies to compete against the US in such a short period of time?

One possible explanation (though not the only one) was how the US changed its approach to research and development (R&D) funding. In the immediate post-war period, the US government was active in supporting R&D. Between 1953 and 1967 overall R&D increased 350 per cent while government outlays increased 425 per cent. By 1967, the rate of increase in R&D expenditures decreased dramatically with outlays for basic research taking the greatest cut, a 15 per cent decline between 1968 and 1976 (Smith 1990: 81). This trend is explicit in Figure 4.1. While the ratio of US R&D/GNP declined through the middle 1970s, the ratios for Japan and West Germany increased and even surpassed that of the US.

Figure 4:1 Research and Development Expenditures as a Percentage of GNP (1972 US$)

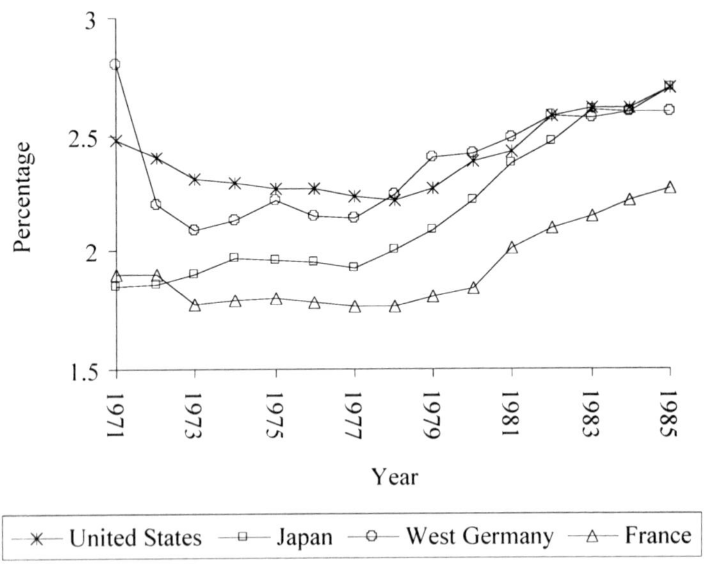

Source: *National Science Foundation*

Equally importantly was *where* the expenditures by sector were allocated. In particular, non-defense R&D expenditures slowed and even declined (Figure 4.2). For Japan and West Germany, these expenditures rose throughout this period. Of course, it was easier for

Japan and West Germany to accomplish this because the US had undertaken the defense burdens of both countries.

Explaining the decline in research commitment also requires looking at the US political role in the world. US foreign policy obligations siphoned away money that had been allocated for R&D. In the post-war period, the US assumed responsibility for global military and economic security against perceived communist expansionism. The US anti-communism role in the world directly led the US into the Vietnam War. It is not a coincidence that the rate of R&D expenditures decreased at the height of the Vietnam conflict. In 1964, the number of US personnel committed in Southeast Asia was a mere 23,000, but by 1969 that number had exploded to 543,000. Increased foreign policy expenditures, when coupled with Lyndon Johnson's Great Society program expenditures, took their toll in other national budgetary areas. But the consequences of the 1960s were not limited to fiscal issues.

Figure 4:2 Non-Defense Research Expenditures as a Percent of GNP

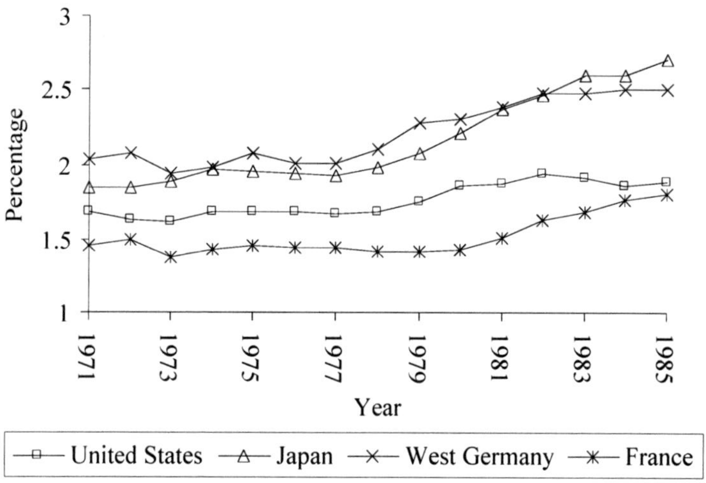

Source: *National Science Foundation*

Campus turmoil in the 1960s also contributed to the decline in R&D commitment. As the pace of R&D expenditures decreased, tensions between faculty and administration and between public and private universities rose. The greatest impact was at universities where ROTC students and Department of Defense research funding came under protest. The growth of campus social protests over Vietnam and other social issues created a chasm of mistrust between universities and the government, upsetting the formerly strong university science-government relationship (Smith 1990: 73-75).

The US global problems were not limited to Vietnam. Though the increase in economic competition showed in the 1960s, the main effects of this were not seen until the early 1970s when the US faced perhaps its greatest short term economic crisis ever: the first oil shock. By 1973, Western economies were dependent on oil to generate economic growth. Since the 1950s, the Arab countries, and particularly Saudi Arabia under King Faisal, had threatened to use the "oil weapon" to change the direction of US policy in the Middle East. Arab countries had perceived the US as being, at least publicly, too "pro-Israel." But Faisal was worried about the spread of communism in the Middle East and was thus reluctant to use the weapon for fear of damaging the close relationship he maintained with the US. But intense lobbying pressure from Egypt's President Anwar Sadat convinced Faisal to change his policy direction.

Sadat had come to the conclusion that Egypt needed to change the situation in the Middle East. Egypt was spending close to 20 per cent of its GNP on the military, making economic progress in the country virtually impossible. At the same time, Sadat perceived his negotiating position with the Israelis as weak because the Israelis occupied the east bank of the Suez Canal after the 1967 war. He ultimately concluded that war was the only solution to his problem (Yergin 1991: 593). On October 6, 1973, in a surprise attack, Egyptian troops launched a full scale invasion of Israel across the Sinai desert while Syrian troops crossed the Golan Heights from the north.

The war unfolded quite quickly with Arab troops making substantial gains against the Israelis. Israel needed US support quickly as defeat in the war was rapidly approaching. But the US was concerned about upsetting the Arabs and the Soviets, making direct assistance a risky proposition. The US decided to supply Israel covertly, sending supplies under the cover of darkness. However, delays caused the supplies to arrive in broad daylight, revealing the operation. Faisal warned the US to stop its activities in helping Israel. Henry Kissinger reassured the Saudis that the resupply was not anti-Arab but instead should be viewed in the context of the US-USSR rivalry. But on October 19, Nixon proposed US$2.2 billion military aid package for Israel, prompting Faisal to order a total embargo of Saudi oil against the US (Yergin 1991: 588-609).

The results of the first oil shock were staggering to American political and corporate leaders. Economic power in the world apparently had shifted against the US. The immediate short-term fallout was the fear of direct investment in the US. Arab resources from the increase in oil prices sparked fears in the US Congress of Arab financial power being used for political and economic influence in the US. Members of Congress proposed a series of bills directed at limiting foreign direct investment in the US. This brought the executive branch, which opposed the bills, directly into conflict with those in the Congress who supported the bills (Pastor 1980: 238-243). Beyond the immediate issue, the oil crisis also solidified, in the eyes of Congress, the perceived decline of the US in political and economic power. Industry leaders also pushed this perception.

The oil shocks also affected American industry. Prior to 1970, corporations produced a steady profits yearly simply by raising prices (Harrison and Bluestone 1988: 22). But as markets opened to foreign competition and imports increased, the old way of profit-making went to the wayside. Corporate leaders could not afford to raise prices in the new competitive environment. As Figure 4:3 shows, corporate profits in the US stagnated in the late 1960s and again in the mid-1970s. Merchandise imports were slightly less than exports through the late 1960s, but in the early 1970s the tide had turned and imports began to surpass exports by increasingly larger margins (Figure 4:4). This shift occurred because industrialized countries managed to make major inroads into American domestic markets (Harrison and Bluestone 1988: 8).

Figure 4:3 Corporate Profits, 1959-1995 (Billions US$)

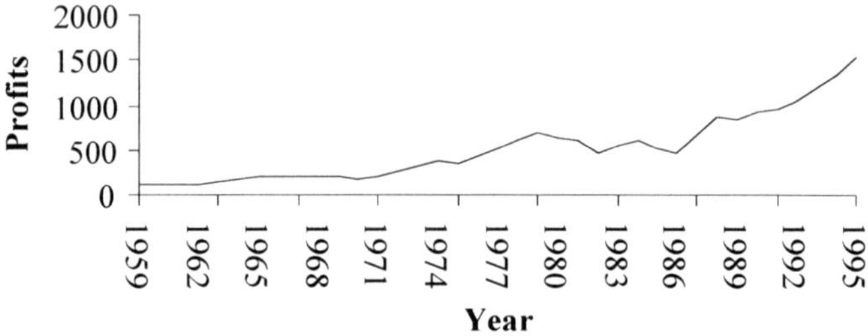

Source: *DRI*

The alternative profit-increasing mechanism for corporate leaders was to substitute cheaper materials in the production process. For example, in the auto industry, plastic was substituted for steel where possible. The first oil shock, however, negated these gains, as petroleum is a key ingredient in plastic production (Harrison and Bluestone 1988: 23). Corporate managers also tried making short term cost reductions instead of long-term technological investments and cutting labor costs by establishing production facilities overseas, hiring cheaper labor and buying cheaper foreign parts (Harrison and Bluestone 1988: 25). Despite these changes, corporate America still faced the same inescapable problem: global competition.

Figure 4:4 Merchandise Imports and Exports (Current US$)

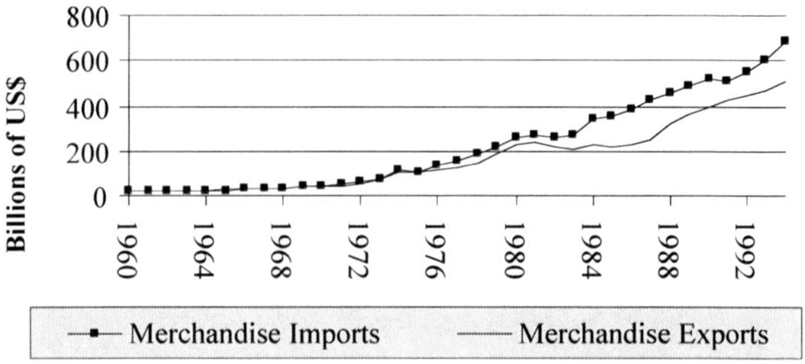

Source: World Bank

In short, America showed signs of "decline." America's "decline," however, was not in absolute terms, but in relative terms. By the 1970s the US could no longer supply all the military and economic security for all its allies while simultaneously competing against them in international economic markets. With the rise of foreign competition, industries asserted their parochial interests by turning to the one entity that could alleviate the new competitive bite: the federal government. Trade deficits due to larger imports increased the political viability for claims that American firms faced unfair international competition. As Destler observed, "Once we equated negative trade figures with a decline of the United States, it was more comfortable to blame this on foreign nefariousness than on domestic inadequacies" (Destler 1992: 50).

Responding to the US "Decline"

The scene was set for another clash between the historically protectionist Congress, eager to support special interests, and the *laissez faire* presidency, fighting for more markets and greater American access to them. Protectionist forces in the Congress, however, had been pressing for trade restrictions since the late 1960s. Recognizing the pressure and the need for a new direction in trade policy, the Nixon administration submitted to the Congress a comprehensive bill requesting unprecedented negotiating power in international trade issues for the President. But with Watergate and Vietnam hovering over Nixon, Congress was not eager to enhance the power of this president in any capacity. Ultimately, after working out differences between the two branches, Congress passed the Trade Act of 1974. In this legislation, the US adopted a two-track trade policy that later became the foundation for current US IPR trade policies. In particular, the Trade Act of 1974 revised Section 337 of the Trade Act of 1930 and replaced Section 252 of the Trade Act of 1962 with the new Section 301 of the 1974 law.

Track I: Section 337—the Import Track

Track I of the revamped US trade policy was Section 337, which was designed originally to protect industry from a broad range of unfair practices and focused on the import side of US trade. Section 337 of the 1930 act contained three sections of importance: 337(a), 337(b) and 337(c). Section 337(a) declared unlawful the importation of products into the US that injured or destroyed established industries or restricted or monopolized trade (Campbell 1976: 674). Section 337(b) authorized the Tariff Commission (renamed the International Trade Commission) to investigate complaints of unfair imports. Section 337(c) guaranteed that the Tariff Commission would transmit the results of its investigations to the president. If the president found the existence of unfair practices, he was required to exclude those products from import into the US (Campbell 1976: 675). In this sense, Section 337(c) gave the president a veto over the commission's findings, enhancing the president's power in trade matters. The principal use of Section 337 was in blocking patent infringing items from being imported into the US (Campbell 1976; Newman 1989; Mutti 1993).

Track II: Section 301— The Export Track

Congress designed Section 301 to be used as a tool to assure fair and adequate access to foreign markets for US export products. The predecessor to Section 301, Section 252 of the Trade Expansion Act of 1962, was, in the opinion of Congress, underutilized and ineffective. Under Section 252, when countries impeded entry of US exports to their markets, the law authorized the president to pursue four specific points:

> Take steps to eliminate the impediment
> Suspend product concessions in any trade agreement with that country
> Not enter into any agreements with that country concerning the product in question
> For restrictions and duties on agricultural products, the president was required to reciprocate (Campbell 1976: 652-3).

Under these provisions, the president had limited authority. The law only authorized him either to suspend concessions or not to enter into any further agreements with the offending country. As Campbell notes, a serious effort was made in the 1962 legislation to keep the provisions consistent with the global trade regime, the General

Agreement on Tariffs and Trade (Campbell 1976: 652). In the 1974 Act, the administration sought a major expansion of the President's authority.

Section 301 differed from Section 252 in two important ways. First, and perhaps most importantly, it expanded the president's power to deal with "unreasonable" and "unjustifiable" foreign restrictions on US commerce.[2] Second, while reciprocity under Section 252 was limited to agricultural products, Section 301 set no restrictions, allowing the President to retaliate against unfair trade practices across all exported products.

The Trade Act of 1974: Impact and Implications

As Dhar (1992) argued, the Trade Act of 1974 introduced a new aspect of policy designed to promote exports by demanding that trading partners accept more goods in which the US had a competitive advantage. The US used its economic strength to force open markets for US exports. The intent was clear, as the Senate Finance Committee stated upon passage of the bill: "The Committee does not intend that this 'retaliatory authority' be a dead letter. Foreign trading partners should know that we are willing to do business with them on a fair and free basis, but if they insist on maintaining unfair advantages, swift and certain retaliation against their commerce will occur" (United States Code 1974: 7302-7303). The Congress armed the administration with the authority to protect US markets overseas, but how effective were Section 337 and Section 301?

The short answer is that they were not as effective as had been hoped by all parties concerned with the trade issues, especially those interested in IPR. Section 337, though broadly construed to cover unfair import practices, was utilized most often to protect IP. In fact, most cases filed with the United States International Trade Commission (USITC) under Section 337 were IPR cases. These cases generally were successful for plaintiffs. Of the 221 IPR cases filed with the USITC, only five were dismissed with a negative finding for the plaintiff (Sloan 1990: 309). On the surface, Section 337 seemed to work, but that did not mean it was a problem-free process. In fact Section 337 worked effectively to the extent that the president would allow. The president did not have to accept all USITC Section 337 recommendations. A typical USITC exclusion order issued in favor of a plaintiff can be vetoed by the president.

For example, Texas Instruments (TI) brought a 1987 Section 337 case against Samsung's exports of DRAM (Dynamic Random Access Memory) chips. The USITC ruled in favor of TI, finding that Samsung had violated TI's US patent on DRAM chips. President Reagan, however, rejected the exclusion order. Officially, he considered the order too broad; unofficially, the President had trade and political reasons for rejecting the USITC's recommendations (Fusco 1997). For affected industries, this was a problem in the implementation of the law. Statutory problems also appeared later, including the protection of emerging industries and the enforcement of the exclusion orders by US Customs agents (Subcommittee on Oversights and Investigations of the Committee on Energy and Commerce 1983).

Section 301 cases produced a different result. Similar to Section 337, Section 301 was worded broadly by the Congress to cover a number of government practices that could be construed as unreasonable or unjustifiable. But the number of cases, and specifically IP cases, was relatively small. From 1975 to 1988, plaintiffs filed seventy cases under Section 301 with the United States Trade Representative (USTR). In most cases, the degree of trade liberalization achieved under the subsequent proceedings was marginal. In fact, it was not until 1985 that the USTR accepted the first IPR dispute case to pursue under Section 301 (Case 301-50 against South Korea). As Bayard and Elliott argued, the problem was not with the legislation, but instead with the intransigence of the administration (Bayard and Elliott 1994: 15-16). The most significant problem faced by those seeking Section 301 protection was the reluctance of the executive branch to pursue an activist trade policy that would effectively utilize Section 301 provisions. The president's historical commitment to free trade policies made Section 301 investigation undesirable. Presidents perceived Section 301 to be protectionist in nature, causing them to shy away from using the statute's power. This problem continued well into the 1980s before Congress exerted pressure for a more activist trade policy.

The Trade Act of 1974 marked a significant new era in American trade policy. Through a combination of non-tariff barriers (Section 337) and aggressive export promotion (Section 301), US lawmakers increased US trade protectionism. Some have argued that the policies of the era were mercantilist, promoting exports while curbing imports (Dhar 1992: 12). But while the legislative goals may have been mercantilist, the results of the policy hardly reflected the goal. As noted earlier, merchandise imports soared after the 1974 legislation while exports grew at a more modest pace (see Figure 4:4).

In retrospect, America's economic position in the post-war era changed internationally and domestically, but it was obvious that the two were linked. At the international level, interdependence and pluralism had crept up on the US, challenging its dominant role in the world economy (Spero 1977: 72). States had grown to be mutually, though not equally, dependent upon each other. Domestic markets in the US became saturated and foreign markets grew in importance in order to continue economic and industrial growth. At the same time, new actors in the international economy appeared. Pluralism increased levels of competition not been seen by US industry in the post-war period. Some industry leaders argued that the increased competition resulted from unfair trade practices and sought assistance from the federal government. Lawmakers accepted the unfair trade practices argument as a matter both of short-term expediency and of serving special political interests.

How did these changes affect US industry concern for the protection of their IPR in foreign markets? The IPR problem has its origin in the global and domestic changes the US underwent. As US lawmakers sounded the unfair competition alarms in the promotion of exports, US IPR-dependent industries joined the unfair trade practices bandwagon by accusing foreign governments of creating non-tariff barriers to trade by not properly protecting *foreign* IPR. Researchers have argued that industry interests forced the IPR issue onto the US trade agenda both at the domestic and international levels (Nogues 1990; Schwab 1994; Sell 1995). In general, three industries have been cited as influential in addressing the IPR issue with the US government: pharmaceuticals, software, and the entertainment industry. These industries all experienced the rise of global competition and the spread of technology that facilitated piracy of their products, which contributed to their decision to bring IPR to the US trade agenda. However, the IPR issue evolved differently in each of these industries.

The Pharmaceutical Industry

The pharmaceutical industry tends to rely on patents more than other industries for the protection of its IP. In recent years, the industry has not garnered a favorable reputation with the American public nor with the international community. This reputation has made it difficult to convince national leaders, particularly in the developing world, that patent protection is important to the industry. The reliance on the patent system for protection became a more pressing issue as a result of a series of events in the US and abroad.

The modern American pharmaceutical industry developed at the end of WWI as a result of events that led to the US government's confiscation of German assets, including patents, under the Alien Property Custodian Act of 1917. These assets, including the patents, were sold to American corporations (Noonan 1990: 267). Investors seeking the infusion of know-how into the industry increased funding for research throughout the following two decades. By the 1940s and 1950s, the "glory days" of the pharmaceutical industry emerged with the discovery of sulfonamides, antibiotics, hormones, psychotropics, and vaccines (Noonan 1990; Silverman, Lydecker et al. 1992).[3] By 1948, the American Medical Association recognized the need for patenting pharmaceutical products and rescinded its objection to the practice, citing growing research costs. But the rising research costs were associated directly with the early crises of the industry.

The first crisis for the pharmaceutical industry occurred in 1938 when hundreds of children died after consuming a combination of sulfanilamide and diethylene glycol (antifreeze), a poison. Toxicity tests typically were not completed before marketing the products (Nogues 1990). This incident led to the Food, Drug and Cosmetics Act of 1938, which required applications for new drugs to be submitted to the Food and Drug Administration (FDA) for approval (Nogues 1990: 91). Despite the new regulations, the number of drugs and consequently the amount of profits increased markedly (Figure 4:5) (Silverman, Lydecker et al. 1992: 45). But the "glory days" of the industry would come to a grinding halt.

Figure 4:5 Number of Drugs Introduced in the US, 1940-1979

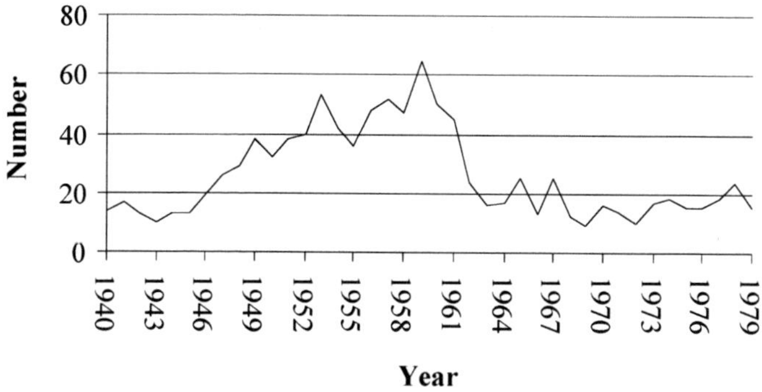

Source: Silverman, M., M. Lydecker, et al. 1992. *Bad Medicine: The Prescription Drug Industry in theThird World.* Stanford: Stanford University Press.

The Kefauver-Nelson hearings of 1962, conducted by Senators Estes Kefauver and Gaylord Nelson, began as in investigation into the market abuses of the pharmaceutical industry. The Senators uncovered the close and cozy relationship between the industry and organized medicine, medical journals, and drug distributors. Additional information about the marketing practices of these companies and European companies in the developing world was also uncovered. Exaggerations of the efficacy of some drugs and the concealment of the hazards of others was routine (Silverman, Lydecker et al. 1992). What the hearings uncovered irreversibly damaged the industry.

The bad news for pharmaceutical firms continued when, just prior to the Congressional hearings, a German physician linked the drug thalidomide to children born with phocomelia, a deformity of the arms and legs. Before its removal, thalidomide was responsible for producing 10,000 cases of phocomelia in twenty countries. Though the drug was never approved in the US, samples were given to physicians, who often gave it to their pregnant wives to ease morning sickness.

As a result of the thalidomide incident and the Kefauver-Nelson hearings, Congress passed the Kefauver-Harris amendment to the 1938 FDA Act. The new amendment repealed the sixty-day approval period for new drugs, required proof of efficacy tests, and established FDA regulatory control over the industry (Nogues 1990). Consequently, the number of new drugs that entered the market plummeted after 1962 (Figure 4:5). Furthermore, the average cost of developing a new drug rose from US$1.7 million in 1962 to US$11.5 million just a decade later (Silverman, Lydecker et al. 1992: 46). While superficially it would appear that the regulations hurt the industry, those same regulations have also produced a competitive advantage for the industry overseas by securing a reputation for safety and efficacy (Pirt 1987: 262).

One drawback, however, was that increased regulations brought about an effective decrease in patent protection. Because pharmaceutical firms needed to file for patent protection prior to the FDA approval process, the effective time for the patent life decreased. While the FDA was spending on average between five and eight years to approve drugs, companies could not actively market the drug, decreasing the time they had to recoup their profits under the patent term. The approval process, some have argued, decreased profits for the industry (Nogues 1990; Silverman, Lydecker et al. 1992). Furthering the alleged profit losses was the introduction of generic drug competition to the market. In 1984, the US Congress passed the Patent Restoration Act. The purpose was twofold: to help brand-name pharmaceutical firms recover some of their patent time and to lessen the burden in getting generic drugs approved. The Act allowed brand-name firms to reclaim up to five years of a drug's patent life lost due to government red tape. It also simplified the FDA regulations for the approval of generic drugs.

At about this same time, some individual states eliminated anti-substitution laws, giving consumers a choice between brand names and generics (Wheaton 1986: 438; Nogues 1990: 94-95; Silverman, Lydecker et al. 1992: 65-66). Generic producers were able to capture a piece of the pharmaceuticals market in the US and abroad. The brand-name companies fought back, claiming that generics were inferior, contaminated, or posed a serious health risk to patients. For example, the pharmaceutical firm Sandoz publicly stated that generic versions of its schizophrenia drug Mellaril were not equivalent to generics and posed a danger to patients. Likewise, Hoechst-Roussel Pharmaceuticals sent thousands of letters to doctors warning them that generic versions of its high blood pressure drug Lasix were potentially dangerous to patients. The FDA declared both claims to be unsubstantiated or untrue (Silverman, Lydecker et al. 1992: 68). Under FDA pressure, the disinformation campaign slowed. Generics eventually took up to one-fourth of the US market for drugs while the brand-name companies argued that the increased competition was depleting their research funds. The ironic part of this claim is that brand-name firms marketed about 80 per cent of the generic drugs (Silverman, Lydecker et al. 1992: 69).

Despite their claims, it is unclear that the pharmaceutical industry faced dramatic domestic competition increases. Some argued that there were indeed profit losses (Nogues 1990; Silverman, Lydecker et al. 1992), while others contended that earnings for the industry were well above those for other manufacturing industries and were expected to grow indefinitely (Pirt 1987: 270). However one interprets the issue, the pharmaceutical industry at least wanted the public to perceive that it was losing money.

Though the claim of increased domestic competition may be dubious, the competition faced by pharmaceutical firms globally was certainly undeniable. Two factors contributed to the competition: the dismal reputation of the industry in the developing world and attempts by developing countries to break their dependence on developed-world pharmaceuticals. In fact, in both cases, the pharmaceutical industry seemed to be its own worst enemy. Overall, multinational and local drug industries garnered a reputation for using bribes, threats, and political influence to keep their products on the market or to be permitted the use of unsubstantiated product promotional material.

Aside from political tactics, the unethical marketing of drugs contributed to the industry's poor reputation overseas. For example, the drug Lomotil was used to control severe diarrhea, a dangerous condition in developing countries. In the US, the drug was not recommended for use by children because of its toxicity; the difference between a correct dosage and a fatal dosage was only slight (Pirt 1987: 273). The manufacturer marketed Lomotil in Sudan, boasting that it had been used by astronauts of Gemini and Apollo and that children as young as one would benefit greatly (Pirt 1987: 273). Other stories have contributed to the general reputation of the pharmaceutical firms, including the present-day distribution of thalidomide in developing countries.

The industry has attempted to repair its damaged reputation through several methods, including the distribution of free drugs to developing countries. But even this venture tarnished the reputation of the industry. A recent example involved Eli Lilly and its antibiotic drug CecloCd. In 1994, as Rwandan refugees fled the civil war, Eli Lilly announced that it had made the largest product donation in its history, six million pills of CecloCd to help "in times of human tragedy" (Purvis 1996). The gift seemed too good to be true—and it was. The World Health Organization (WHO) did not list CecloCd on its vital drugs list. The leading relief group in the area, Doctors without Borders, said that the drug could build immune resistance to other more valuable drugs in the region. Despite all these issues, the drugs were sent and aid workers had to dispose of them as quickly as they arrived.

This practice of sending worthless drugs or expired drugs to developing countries became commonplace. The WHO estimates 45 per cent of the drugs received in Yugoslavia during its civil war were worthless. In Rwanda, garlic pills, ginseng extract and antacid tablets arrived. A case of cruel irony unfolded when civil war and famine wracked Sudan; the drug firms sent contact lens solution and appetite suppressants (Purvis 1996). Drug companies actively engaged in these practices to obtain benefits. In some cases, it was to rid themselves of expiring medicines that occupied shelf space and cost money to dispose of. In others, it was to reap huge tax breaks for donating drugs (Purvis 1996). The result was to shift pharmaceutical industry problems to the developing world, turning some countries and refugee camps into chemical waste dumps.

Developing countries faced with these problems attempted to develop indigenous drug industries. Beginning in the 1950s, several countries began developing industries but struggled because of the lack of available resources. Reliance on drug imports continued, but progress was made in some countries. Some countries, such as Brazil, Argentina, Mexico, India, Cuba and South Korea, joined the ranks of drug-producing countries (Wortzel 1971; Silverman, Lydecker et al. 1992). In some cases, these countries also began exporting drugs, providing additional competition in the global markets for US firms. But the most important aspect of overseas markets for the US pharmaceutical industry was in how some of these foreign industries evolved through the duplication of existing technologies or what the US pharmaceutical producers deemed to be patent infringement and piracy (an ironic claim given the origins of the US pharmaceutical industry). Developing countries justified the duplication of existing drugs on cultural, ethical and economic grounds.

The piracy issue grew in importance for the US pharmaceutical industry because foreign based subsidiaries had increased dramatically. The increase in foreign subsidiaries was tied to the increase in US domestic regulations and the generally lax regulations of other countries. In 1960, overseas subsidiary sales as a percentage of total sales amounted to 20.6 per cent, but by 1979 that figure had nearly doubled and in some cases exceeded 50 per cent, indicating that the US pharmaceutical industry had become more dependent on foreign markets for sales (Pirt 1987: 267). But as domestic drug industries grew in developing countries, so did the alleged losses to the US industry. Foreign pharmaceutical firms continued to copy existing drugs for their domestic markets. Drug companies in the developing world were able to keep prices relatively low, discouraging dangerous attempts to counterfeit the drugs on the market. For example, in India, drug prices were five to thirty-five times lower than in other retail markets and compared to the US, prices were 900 to 3010 times lower (May 1991: 46). But the net effect for the US pharmaceutical industry was a rise of "unfair" competition in international markets and in domestic markets of developing countries, which had become an important revenue source.

The Computer Software Industry

The computer software industry and the entertainment industry (discussed later) are different cases than the pharmaceutical industry. Both these industries do not produce life extending or life saving products, though in some cases they do produce items that may aid in that goal. The computer industry, and particularly the software industry, has taken on an important role in the lives of Americans and others. But the spread of computers and software has also led to complex issues that break new legal ground, from copyrights and patents to free speech.

The software industry evolved into a global giant in a short period of time. Compared to other industries, it is still in its infancy. But in this brief time, the industry has had a global impact like no other in history. Its growth is a combination of several factors that in many ways are unique to the US. The size and diversity of the domestic market in the US has been the driving force behind the industry's growth, while other factors such as industrial diversification and innovation have also contributed significantly (Siwek and Furchtgott-Roth 1993).

Culturally driven market factors also have contributed to the industry's success. Software and accompanying manuals are written mostly in English code. While they can be translated into other languages, it is unprofitable to do so unless a large market exists for the product. It may not be feasible to translate some programs into Luganda because of the relatively small size of the software market in Uganda. But the translation of programs into Mandarin for Chinese consumers may prove to be a major financial windfall for software companies. Larger consumer markets provide considerable incentives to translate software, mitigating the additional costs associated with producing the programs in multiple languages. Because the US had the lead position in the software market, the majority of software in the world was written in English. The additional expenses in producing translated versions of software means many programs are written in English and sold only in English versions because small software firms, which make up the bulk of the US software industry, cannot undertake the additional expenses.

Computer hardware was the dominant product in the early stages of the industry's development. Designers constructed computers with a common architecture to promote software compatibility between systems and between generations of new computers. Software could be transferred from one system to another or from one generation of computers to the next without modification (Band and Katoh 1995: 18). The world's leading computer maker at the time, IBM, expected hardware to be the primary profit-maker. But because of antitrust litigation brought in the early 1970s, IBM, which had a virtual monopoly on computer production, lost market share to IBM-compatible producers and profits in hardware nosedived.

Though IBM lost part of the hardware market, US court cases and legislation convinced IBM and other producers that copyrights could extend to software. In 1978, IBM began to attach copyrights to its operating system software and charged for its use (Band and Katoh 1995: 25). Copyrighted software later gave birth to the software giant Microsoft, whose president, Bill Gates, had convinced IBM to use his MS-DOS operating system in IBM's computers. That arrangement was easily transferred to the compatibles market, increasing profits substantially for the upstart software company (Wallace and Erickson 1992; Engardio and Roberts 1996).

IBM furiously entered into litigation against those that used its software or hardware without consent. IBM's zealous enforcement of copyrights coincided with a revision of antitrust theory at the Department of Justice. Instead of conceiving some licensing practices of IP as antitrust violations, the Antitrust Division began viewing IP as another asset, similar to tangible property. The owners were thus entitled to enjoy the market power they acquired through sales of their property (Band and Katoh 1995: 44). The new interpretation produced a deluge of litigation as IBM, Apple, Texas Instruments, Microsoft, Lotus, and other developers sued and counter-sued each other and other producers for copyright infringement throughout the 1980s.

With the expansion of the domestic software market, producers faced another form of copyright violation: piracy. To combat piracy, software producers formed the Software Publishers Association. The organization's goals were to lobby for better protection of software and to educate the public about the issue (Marshall 1993: 441). Domestic abuses consisted mostly of corporate users who purchased software and passed it along to co-workers or made multiple copies for in-house use. The other major form of piracy was the growing number of bulletin boards designed specifically to exchange copyrighted software. Through the organization's work, the incidence of corporate violations generally declined (Marshall 1993: 446).

By the late 1980s, the US software industry had solidified its domestic base and sought expansion to newly emerging markets, particularly in Asia, where industry growth forecasts were promising. It was not long before the software industry would dominate foreign markets, while at the same time, the new markets became increasingly more important to the industry. Sales in foreign markets had accounted for nearly half of all sales by 1991 (Table 4:2). Foreign markets such as India also became important for outsourcing.[4] As the developed countries experienced shortages in software programmers, firms began to outsource the work to countries with low-cost labor (Heeks 1996: 110-111).

As overseas markets flourished, software piracy grew. Large corporations became active in pursuing large copyright infringers on their own. Microsoft was instrumental in providing Chinese government officials with information that broke up a piracy ring in the south China city of Guilin. The pirates had been producing over 20,000 CD-ROMS a day (Engardio and Roberts 1996: 54). The profitability of software piracy has also brought new, unsavory players into the market—organized crime. In raids sponsored by producers Apple, Autodesk, Lotus, Microsoft and Ashton-Tate, police launched a 1989 raid of the Golden Arcade, Hong Kong's leading retail center for pirated software. The raids netted US$350 million in pirated retail computer software. But the interesting aspects of this case were the quality of the copies, the professional manuals, and the use of technologically advanced equipment. Investigators speculated that only the six syndicates tied to the triads (the Chinese Mafia) would spend the amount of money required for this type of piracy operation. While software piracy is typically geared for individual consumers, the targeted market in this instance was *corporations* (Skrentny 1989: 42).

Table 4:2 Foreign Sales of US Software, 1986-1991 (billions of US$)*

	Total Software Sales	Foreign Software Sales	Percent Non-US Sales
1986	$3.8	$0.9	23.7%
1987	$5.2	$2.2	42.3%
1989	$8.3	$3.7	44.6%
1990	$10.7	$4.9	45.8%
1991	$12.5	$6.0	48.0%

*Data for 1988 were not available. Source: Economists Incorporated, from a survey commissioned by the Business Software Alliance, in (Marshall 1993: 446).

Fighting the software pirates thus took on both foreign and domestic theaters of operation. Domestically, software producers had the problem under control, particularly after the passage of legislation under the Bush administration that made software piracy a felony (Marshall 1993: 441). The next phase was to get the foreign governments to take the issue seriously as well. For this, the software industry turned to the US government to address the issue in trade fora.

The Entertainment Industry

Prior to the 1980s, the US entertainment industry had a solid base in foreign markets; Hollywood USA had little real competition globally. The industry produced and marketed its products without threat of mass illicit duplication. The IP issue for the entertainment industry appeared during the 1980s with the spread of sophisticated, widely-available technology that made duplication of media easier and more economical. Items such as video and audio recorders, compact disc writers and other computer technology hastened the speed and ease at which media could be copied. In protecting their IP, the entertainment industry faced a myriad of issues that the pharmaceutical and software industries did not encounter: unauthorized public exhibition, print theft, videocassette piracy, and broadcast signal theft.

Unauthorized public exhibition became a concern for the industry, especially in European markets (Wildman and Siwek 1988: 102). Much of the infringement occurred when hotels, cafes or "vid-bars" showed copyrighted works in public areas without paying royalties to the producers. Likewise, the theft of film prints also appeared predominantly in European countries. Film prints could be stolen during any number of stages in the distribution process, with a primary source being movie distributors who did not return film copies. The most serious and widespread form of infringement during this period was the copying of videocassettes (Wildman and Siwek 1988: 103). In the mid-1980s, this phenomenon drew concern from the Motion Picture Export Association of America (MPEAA). Several countries provided a tremendous market for pirated videotapes (Table 4:3). But domestic pirates in these countries were not always the source. Countries such as Britain and West Germany made a lucrative profit exporting pirated cassettes around the world (Wildman and Siwek 1988: 103). The losses that the US entertainment industries claimed from foreign pirating were substantial (Table 4:4). Total US trade losses from pirating of movies and videos in Europe alone were US$200 million and possibly as much as US$1 billion worldwide (Wildman and Siwek 1988: 102).

Table 4:3 Estimates of Market Share for Pirated Videocassettes

Percent of Market Share for Pirated Cassettes	Countries
100	Brazil, Colombia, Mexico, Taiwan
65	Spain
60	Netherlands
45	West Germany
40	Ireland
35	Britain, Belgium
30	Austria, Venezuela
20	Australia, Canada, France
12	South Africa
10	Hong Kong, Italy, Japan

Source: MPEAA, Report to the United States Trade Representative: Trade Restrictions Facing US Film producers Abroad (Washington, DC: MPEAA, April 4, 1985) in (Wildman and Siwek 1988: 103).

Table 4:4 Estimated US Trade Losses 1993 (Millions of US$)

	Movies	Music	Software	Books	Total
Brazil	50	10	40	25	125
Cyprus	32	4		15	51
Egypt	37	4	14	15	70
El Salvador	1.4	5		1	7.4
Greece	37	21		4	62
Guatemala	1.1			1	2.1
Hungary	25	11		4	40
India	40	41	63	25	169
Indonesia	40	16		40	96
Italy	224	38	238		500
P.R. China	45	45	225	100	415
Pakistan	20			20	40
Philippines	15	5	25	70	115

Table 4:4 Cont.

	Movies	Music	Software	Books	Total
Poland	45	30	100	15	190
Saudi Arabia	50	33	28	6	117
South Korea	20	66	315	15	416
Spain	31	7	336		374
Taiwan	45	24	585	15	669
Thailand	30	24	49	20	123
Turkey	35	12	55	15	117
U.A.E.	6	108		2	116
Venezuela	12	10	40	20	82
Total	*841.5*	*514*	*2113*	*428*	*3897*

Source: International Intellectual Property Alliance in (Marshall 1993: 438)

The final IP issue was the theft of broadcast signals. The problem was most prevalent in developing countries, particularly in the Caribbean where close proximity to the US made theft relatively easy. The theft of the signals occurred in a number of ways, including home viewing of the signal by satellite dish owners, re-transmission of US programming by local television stations, redistribution by local cable companies, and recording of programs on video cassettes for distribution (Wildman and Siwek 1988: 104; Ebanks 1989: 34). In 1989, losses from signal piracy were estimated at US$700 million for the industry (Ebanks 1989: 34). The Motion Picture Association of America (MPAA) claimed such losses were death knells for the industry because only about one-third of its movies actually recovered production costs in distribution (Ebanks 1989: 35).

In 1983, the Reagan administration provided help to the industry in its battle against signal piracy. In determining whether countries could receive benefits under the Caribbean Basin Initiative for Economic Development, the President was required to take into consideration the extent that countries fought signal piracy. However, this measure turned out to be more of a show of the administration's deepening concern over the issue than a real means to stopping piracy (Ebanks 1989: 41).

Fighting foreign piracy became a major issue for the industry. The importance of these markets laid with the rising production costs in the entertainment industry (Wasko 1994: 223). Lucrative star contracts and demands for high-cost special effects increased the money needed for movie production. Foreign markets were instrumental in providing additional revenues (Table 4:5).

Table 4:5 Gross Revenues of Selected Films (Millions US$)

	United States Market	Foreign Markets
Rain Man (MGM/UA)	170	233
Fatal Attraction (Paramount)	157	189
Who Framed Roger Rabbit? (Buena Vista)	154	180
Black Rain (Paramount)	48	52
Cocktail (Disney)	77	89
Frantic (Warner Bros)	17	34

Source: Fabrikant, Geraldine, "When World Raves, Studios Jump," *New York Times*, 7 March 1990 in (Wasko 1994: 223)

To combat all forms of piracy, the industry mounted its own offensive. For example, Jack Valenti, president of the MPAA, entered into talks with South Korea to curb piracy (Sell 1995: 174-75). In fact, Valenti and Richard Mossinghoff, president of the Pharmaceutical Manufacturers Association, both recommended stripping countries of their generalized system of preference (GSP) benefits if IPR protection was not addressed. Hence, the entertainment industry, like the pharmaceutical and software industries, had turned to the US government for trade-based assistance in fighting their IPR problems overseas.

Summary

The common factors influencing each of these three industries' decision to pursue IPR concerns with the US government were the effects of global competition and the spread of technology that posed threats to each industry. What is important to remember though is these industries are especially dependent on IPR protection for their profits. In the pharmaceutical industry, competition from indigenous industries emerged from the spread of reverse-engineering technology that made duplication of drug compounds inexpensive and easy. The software and entertainment industries were victims of their own technology. The same technology that allowed them to make profits also aided in the duplication of their products in foreign markets. As a result, pressure from losses due to piracy mounted. Foreign governments generally were unresponsive to the concerns the industries raised. The last resort for the industries was to turn to the US government. With protectionist sentiments mounting in the Congress during the early 1980s, the time was ripe for industry to bring the issue to the trade agenda.

Ronald Reagan and the Congressional Ghosts of Protectionism Past

Ronald Reagan's election in 1980 marked an important turn for the country, which was suffering from double-digit inflation, high unemployment, and stagnant economic growth. The American voters elected Reagan hoping he could reinvigorate the economy and reestablish America's dominant position in the global economy. Promising free trade, deregulation and tax cuts, Reagan began the Republican supply-side revolution with great fanfare. But the hopes of the electorate faded quickly. Reagan's supply-side tax cuts did not yield the promised economic expansion. With mushrooming budget deficits and high interest rates to combat inflation, the US became a prime target for foreign investment and imports. The rising value of the US dollar promoted an expanding trade deficit as American consumers bought foreign goods (see Figure 4:2). Additionally, the Latin American debt crisis caused a decrease in US exports to the region, exacerbating the trade deficit (Bayard and Elliott 1994: 14). Despite these macroeconomic problems, Congressional protectionist sentiments reemerged, guised in a culture of victim-hood that blamed unfair foreign competition for growing trade deficits and general weakness in the American economy. The administration's reaction to the rising protectionist movement was lukewarm. Aside from a few import measures taken against foreign producers, Reagan was content with a *laissez faire* approach to trade. The problem with this approach was that it did not grapple with the underlying source of the issue (Bayard and Elliott 1994: 15). Reagan's first term and the initial months of his second term were thus characterized by an apparent apathy (Destler 1992: 124-5).

Destler (1992) argued that the administration became its own worst enemy. When business leaders discussed the growing trade deficit and the rise in the dollar's value, the administration turned a deaf ear. According to Reagan, American business needed to be more competitive and less complacent in the face of competition. He rejected industry leaders' pleas for macroeconomic adjustments, forcing business leaders to seek Congressional assistance. Leaders in Congress raised the protectionist banner and as more businesses went to Congress, pressure mounted on the administration to do something about the trade problem. The administration took the warning from Congress and pursued a more activist trade policy in Reagan's second term.

As the trade issue bounced back and forth between the two branches, special interest groups lobbying for greater IPR protection in foreign markets made significant inroads in Congress, with the pharmaceutical and entertainment industries leading the way. In 1983, as trade issues made headlines across the country, Congress took the opportunity to hold high profile hearings on unfair foreign trade practices that culminated in the passage of the 1984 Trade Act. Industries seeking a trade-based approach to the IPR issue aggressively lobbied Congress. The 1984 Trade Act authorized the office of the USTR to initiate investigations of unfair trade practices on its own. Congress also adjusted the definitions of "unreasonable" and "unjustifiable" trade practices to include IPR (Sell 1995: 172). Still, lobbyists continued their battle for tighter foreign IPR protection. Additional assistance came in two administration reports: the first from the President's Commission on Industrial Competitiveness (CIC) and the second from the USTR.

On June 28, 1983, Reagan signed an executive order creating the CIC, which had as its goals to identify problems that industry faced and to recommend policy solutions. The President chose government officials, corporate leaders, and academics as commission members. The CIC cited IPR as a major problem in US trade relations, which was not surprising given the strong representation of high-technology firms on the commission. Half of the CIC report on IPR was dedicated to trade-based IP problems. While the CIC report brought attention to the IPR issue, private industry drew more attention to the issue. In 1984, in a series of confidential memoranda, the Advisory Committee on Trade Negotiations (ACTN) urged the administration to issue a statement on IPR protection that established a solid policy for dealing with foreign violations: a "carrot and stick" approach should be used in which the US rewarded stronger IPR protection with increased technical assistance and aid. Conversely a lack of IPR protection would be punished by restricting access to the US market for those countries that did not protect US IPR (*Inside US Trade* January 24, 1986). As Sell (1995) underscored, representatives of major industrial interests, such as John Opel of IBM, Fritz Attaway of the MPAA, and Abraham Cohen, president of Merck Pharmaceuticals International Division, sat on the ACTN's Task Force for IPR. Hence, the pharmaceutical, computer, and entertainment industries' concerns had stout clout at the highest levels of the federal government. In fact, the ACTN's recommendations were most likely the primary source of the USTR's report on trade-related IPR problems (Sell 1995).

Shortly after the release of the CIC report in 1985, the USTR's office released its own report on the effectiveness of the administration's bilateral approach to IPR issues. Diplomatic wrangling with South Korea, Singapore, and Mexico over IPR-related trade problems had produced few tangible results, prompting a look at the effectiveness of the policy. The USTR, in conjunction with the President's Economic Policy Council, called the administration's bilateral approach to the IPR issue a failure and declared that the administration needed to seriously reconsider its policies. The USTR recommended multilateral, bilateral and unilateral approaches to address the IPR issue, including aggressive use of Section 301 of the 1974 Trade Act and international trade fora (*Inside US Trade* January 24, 1986: 10). While the unilateral approach initially was based on tightening import laws (predominantly through Section 337), the implementation of the other approaches was more complicated.

Gadbaw and Gwynn emphasized the important role of industry in the multilateral approach, noting that "Both the extent and nature of private sector participation in these negotiations [was] unprecedented, and the success of the initiative [was] vitally dependent upon the resourcefulness and effectiveness of these efforts" (Gadbaw and Gwynn 1988: 39). The administration's approach followed industry leaders' suggestions that the IPR issue be brought to the largest trade forum, the General Agreement on Tariffs and Trade (GATT).

Following the CIC's report, which endorsed the multilateral framework, the administration worked to place the IPR issue on the negotiation agenda for the new GATT round.

Industry leaders, including members of the ACTN, saw this as a chance to impose universal IPR standards in all markets and took the opportunity to address the issue in specially arranged meetings with GATT officials. Though the exact topics for the meetings were not released publicly, they most likely included discussions on IPR protection (*Inside US Trade* January 29, 1988). But putting the IPR issue on the GATT agenda would not be easy in the face of resistance from developing countries. India and Brazil led strong opposition. Other developing countries would not reveal their position on the issue, hoping instead to gain bargaining leverage for their own trade issues if IPR were placed on the agenda. Some developing countries considered trading their support for the IPR issue in exchange for other benefits (*Inside US Trade* November 25, 1988: 7)[5]

Despite objections from the developing countries, the US, with the support of its allies, persuaded the full GATT membership to include IPR protection on the agenda for a new GATT Round proclaimed by the Uruguay Round Ministerial Declaration of September 20, 1986. The GATT body formed the Negotiating Group on Trade Related Intellectual Property (TRIPS), but this mandate did not end the protests from developing countries regarding the inclusion of IPR protection on the agenda. The Ministerial Declaration was subject to a variety of interpretations. Brazil's letter of March 25, 1987 to the Negotiating Group on TRIPS illustrated the problems that the group encountered.

> It should be clear to all participants that we are not here to engage in an exercise to set standards of protection of intellectual property rights or to attempt to raise the levels of such protection under existing multilateral agreements through the strengthening of enforcement procedures...Our task here is of [a] totally different nature: that of examining the operation of relevant GATT provisions and of ascertaining...whether or not there is need for clarifying them or for additional disciplines having to do with the effect on trade in goods of the exercise by individual contracting parties of their duty to protect intellectual property rights.[6]

Brazil's active role against including IPR protection on the GATT trade agenda served only to highlight the problems the US government saw in Brazil's weak IPR protection policies. The administration's first opportunity using its bilateral approach to the IPR issue came in a Section 301 case filed against Brazil, which accused the Brazilian government of unfair barriers to entry in the microcomputer industry and inadequate copyright protection for the software industry. After extensive negotiations between the USTR and Brazilian President José Sarney, Sarney rescinded regulations aimed at restricting access to the software industry in September 1986 (*Inside US Trade* October 3, 1986). By the end of 1986, the administration entered a second round of negotiations aimed at easing entry to Brazil's informatics industry, while also opening preliminary investigations into complaints regarding inadequate patent protection for American pharmaceutical products (*Inside US Trade* November 21, 1986). But by April 1987, Congressional leaders grew impatient with the administration's handling of the Section 301 case against Brazil and a Congressional delegation went to Brazil on a fact finding mission. Upon returning, the delegation sent a letter to President Reagan expressing its "grave concern" over the Brazil situation (*Inside US Trade* May 8, 1987). The delegation conveyed concern about several trade issues, including entry into the informatics industry. The letter implied, however, that the reasons for opening Brazil's informatics market went well beyond concern for "fair trade:"

> The Brazilian economy ranks among the ten largest in the world. By employing misappropriated technology and closing its border to meaningful import competition, Brazil is fostering and, indeed, subsidizing the development of a domestic informatics industry which could grow into a formidable competitor with the United States for market share in other countries (*Inside US Trade* May 8, 1987: 9).

Congressional leaders were not only concerned with access to Brazil's domestic market, but also with future competition that Brazil's industry could pose to the US in other markets. After Brazil's government rejected a software licensing agreement with US firms, the administration threatened to impose US$105 million in penalties on Brazil's exports to the US (Bayard and Elliott 1994: 423). Pressure mounted and by the end of 1988 Brazil passed legislation that increased foreign access to its software industry. The Section 301 case against Brazil was dismissed after Brazil passed this legislation, though some issues were left unresolved.

The Section 301 case against Brazil demonstrated two points. First, the administration had adopted a more activist bilateral policy in pursuing trade issues, though not at the pace Congressional leaders had hoped. More importantly, it demonstrated mounting Congressional impatience with the Reagan administration on a series of trade issues and the extent to which members of Congress wanted resolution to them. The prevailing thought in the Congress was that the solution to America's trade deficit problem lay in dealing directly with individual countries to decrease perceived unfair trade practices. Protectionist sentiments grew in the Congress despite a General Accounting Office (GAO) report, released at the height of the trade dispute with Brazil, which maintained unfair foreign trade practices accounted for a negligible part the trade deficit. The major cause of the trade deficit, the GAO concluded, was the rising value of the dollar and the budget deficit, which industry leaders originally tried to address with the administration (Phillips 1989).[7] Despite the GAO report, leaders in Congress called for new legislation to tighten American trade laws against unfair import competition and to open foreign markets for US exports.

The Move to Aggressive Unilateralism

Following the 1986 midterm elections, the Democratic Party recaptured control of both houses of the Congress. Democratic leaders announced that trade would be the number-one issue on their legislative agenda. Congress wanted to reassert control over trade issues and to force action on unfair trade practices (Phillips 1989: 495). The issue also provided a platform for House leader Richard Gephardt (D-MO), who had presidential aspirations. The House wasted no time in addressing the trade issue, submitting HR 4800, the Omnibus Trade Act of 1986. In a sign of events to follow, President Reagan labeled the bill "kamikaze" and unacceptable. The Senate, busy with tax reform, did not have the time to take up the bill, killing the possibility of passage in the 1986 calendar year (Phillips 1989: 498).

In 1987, House leaders reintroduced HR 4800 as HR 3 and quickly approved it. After two months of hearings by the Senate Finance Committee, the bill moved to the Senate floor for a vote, but the administration listed nearly forty objections to the bill in a memorandum to the Senate. Amongst other issues, the administration objected to Section 301 revisions that dealt with IPR protection. The bill mandated a sector-oriented negotiation scheme for countries that did not protect IPR adequately: "While this provision does not mandate any action as a consequence of negotiations, it is special interest legislation, includes mandatory self-initiation of negotiations, and is unnecessary (since Section 301 [of the Trade Act of 1974] already authorizes such negotiations)" (*Inside US Trade* May 22, 1987).[8] Despite the list of objections, the bill passed and went to a conference committee. Reagan later vetoed the bill, citing concerns over plant closings and Alaskan oil provisions (Phillips 1989: 499). Congressional leaders in both Houses resubmitted the bill, excluding the offending provisions. The bill quickly passed both Houses and Reagan signed it without further objections. Known as the Omnibus Trade and Competitiveness Act of 1988, the law reflected protectionist sentiments in Congress while providing IP-dependent industries with the statutory leverage they sought to address foreign IPR protection issues.

Congress made three important changes to Section 301 of the Trade Act of 1974 that fundamentally shifted the pendulum of power on trade issues from the president to the Congress. Retaliatory authority under Section 301 and "Super 301" shifted from the president to the USTR.[9] Congress charged the USTR with (a) deciding whether a practice is actionable or unfair, (b) deciding whether to take action and the action to be taken, and (c) implementing the action within thirty days, subject to presidential direction. The revisions gave Congress more control over retaliatory trade issues because it had the power to call the USTR to committee hearings or to use budget constraints to coerce the USTR to act against unfair trade practices. At the same time, the legislation also strengthened the hand of the USTR, particularly in the interagency Section 301 Committee (Phillips 1989: 511-12).[10]

Once a country was identified as a "problem," the Section 301 Committee met to decide whether to recommend to the president that action be taken under Section 301 (Phillips 1989: 511-512; Anonymous

Personal Interview March 27, 1997). Often, political and diplomatic considerations would override trade considerations, leading to interagency strife that bound the president's hands and delayed action (Phillips 1989: 512; Anonymous Personal Interview March 27, 1997). Congress hoped to eliminate this problem and to smooth the process by giving the USTR the decision to take action, subject to consultations with other agencies. This change also strengthened the USTR's negotiating power with foreign governments (Phillips 1989). Foreign governments often circumvented the USTR and directly lobbied individual cabinet departments that could stop retaliatory action in the Section 301 Committee (Phillips 1989: 513). But the USTR's office became the only game in town when retaliatory power passed to it, diminishing the role of the other cabinet-level players and cutting off foreign lobbies' access to the policy process.

The amended Section 301 also made retaliation mandatory against countries that blocked entry of US exports to their markets. The changes addressed Congress' frustrations on three "related" issues: the administration's inaction in pursuing trade issues, trade deficits and foreign barriers to trade. At the same time, the provisions provided new leverage to US negotiators (Phillips 1989: 514). Knowing that retaliation was the definite outcome gave countries greater incentive to reach a settlement on trade issues. Retaliation was not required if the situation met certain criteria, giving the president some flexibility in negotiations.[11]

The new Special 301 in Omnibus specifically addressed IPR and US retaliation against those countries that did not provide adequate protection. For the most part, these provisions were no different from the Super 301 provisions except that they narrowed the focus to IPR cases. Special 301 required the USTR to determine if the actions of foreign countries denied sufficient protection of IPR or fair and equitable market access for people who rely on IP protection. With the help of public input and information from interested parties such as industries, individual corporations and trade associations, the USTR created a list of countries with inadequate IPR protection. The USTR was then required to categorize these countries into three lists: priority countries, priority watch countries, and watch countries.[12]

The amendment also contained three primary parts for protecting US IPR overseas. First, the USTR had to formulate the list of "priority countries" that had repeated patterns of violating US IPR. Second, the

USTR had to initiate an investigation into the practices of each country to determine if the violations were IPR infringements. If the accusations were valid, the provisions authorized the USTR to attempt a negotiated settlement within thirty days of the valid finding. Third, if the negotiations had not settled the issue within an eighteen-month time period, the provisions mandated the president to take action against the country (Berliner 1990: 735). However, the president had several "loopholes" to escape the retaliation clause.[13] Critics targeted the loopholes, arguing that for political and economic reasons the president or the USTR could delay indefinitely penalties on any country found to be violating US IPR.

Criticism of the Special 301 provisions that specifically addressed IPR protection included strong arguments that the legislation was unnecessary. The powers existed in the 1984 legislation passed by the US Congress (Berliner 1990). Those that made this argument substantiated Reagan's original objection to the legislation when it was in the Senate, which was that its purpose was to serve special interests. Indeed, no other explanation for the legislation existed because the powers given to the president did exist *prior* to the Special 301 legislation.

The new retaliatory provisions of Section 301 also attracted waves of criticism, particularly from foreign governments and academics. Other governments saw this as a form of protectionism, while academics argued that the legislation moved the US toward an aggressively unilateral trade posture that violated GATT rules and exploited weaker trading partners. Probably the most vocal critic was Jagdish Bhagwati who wrote that

> The world trading system should not be built on the assumption that any one player, no matter how dominant, can impose its own rules, unilaterally claiming social legitimacy for them. Institutions cannot be built on notions of benign dictatorship....we must confront the fact that trade policy is rarely made in pluralistic democracies by dictators with monolithic objective functions. Instead, it reflects the resolution of sectional interests in the political domain. There is no necessary correspondence, therefore between the triumphant sectoral interests and the national interests and, most important the international or cosmopolitan interest that

> must define the world trading regime. It is important therefore to reject the view that ... the United States should be permitted to play the roles of self-appointed "trade cop" and "trade czar" (Bhagwati 1990: 37).

Bhagwati's objections to sectoral interests formulating trade policy were directed at the US Congress, which created the climate and the necessary conditions that allowed for protectionist, retaliatory policies to thrive and to be translated into legislation. Congress gave limited consideration to the implications of action under any of the Section 301 provisions. The tools used in unilateral trade action no longer comprised only Section 337 to protect US markets from unfair imports; Congress equipped Section 301 with the necessary provisions to seek out "unfair" foreign trade practices that occurred in *foreign* markets. The provisions allowed the US to bypass international trade fora to address trade grievances and to adopt an "aggressive unilateral" approach to investigating and punishing unfair trade practices.

The Congress had bet on the importance of US markets when it constructed the new Section 301 because it gave little attention to the possibility of counter-retaliation by countries with significant economic power, such as Japan or China. Likewise, Congress did not consider the domestic politics of many countries when it crafted Section 301 (Phillips 1989). As Treasury Secretary James Baker said at Section 301 hearings, the mandatory retaliation of the provision makes states "more likely to dig in and counterattack" while arousing nationalist and anti-American sentiments that could make issue settlement more difficult and possibly worsen trade relations overall (Phillips 1989: 525). As Phillips observed, Korean protestors met attempts by the US to increase tobacco exports to South Korea with a flood of protests denouncing the move as the "US exporting cancer" (Phillips 1989: 525). Congress gave the president few options in handling such issues.

Finally, the new laws gave no consideration to charges of protectionism against the US. For years, European allies and other countries complained that US laws discriminated against foreign products. These countries cited such practices as the "Buy American" provisions in trade and government procurement legislation, sugar and peanut quotas, agricultural subsidies, Section 337, and fishing laws as unfair trade practices in a number of fora. The Congress actually strengthened some of these provisions and laws, particularly Section

337, when it passed Omnibus, following the pattern established in the early 1970s of restricting imports and demanding greater access to export markets from trading partners.

The Move to Aggressive Unilateralism: The Payoff

Success rates under the new Section 301 were similar to those after Congress passed the original legislation in 1974—marginal at best. The legislation opened some markets while also producing no change in others. While Bayard and Elliott showed that the aggressive unilateral US policy was successful in some cases, the net trade gains were marginal, accounting for about US$4 billion dollars in total exports over the entire 1975-1994 period (Bayard and Elliott 1994). These figures hardly reflected the boom to exports that Congressional leaders sought and were instead more reflective of the assessment of the trade deficit presented in the GAO report on unfair foreign trade practices. Of the 91 Section 301 cases documented by Bayard and Elliott since 1974, about ten per cent were IPR cases. The resolution of these cases was nominally successful for the US where at least promises for IPR reform from the targeted countries were negotiated; however, countries often failed to implement the changes to the full satisfaction of the US (Bayard and Elliott 1994: 62-64). Bayard and Elliott also found little evidence of counter-retaliation. In fifteen of the ninety-one cases, retaliation was ordered by the administration, while the target country retaliated in only two cases.

Bayard and Elliott also noted that the total number of Section 301 cases dropped after 1989, but the number of IPR cases filed under Section 301 *doubled* (from three, over the prior four years, to six). The drop in total Section 301 cases reflected the relative satisfaction of non-IPR dependent industries with the export conditions during the 1991-1994 economic expansion, but the increase in IPR cases reflected IPR-dependent industries' dissatisfaction with protection in foreign markets.

With Republicans taking control of both Houses in the 1994 midterm elections and the general economic expansion of the 1990s, protectionist sentiments in the Congress subsided. The Clinton Administration worked closely with the Republican Congress to address significant trade issues. Despite the changed environment between the executive and legislative branches, neither side seemed willing to eliminate the Janus-face of US trade policy that advocated both protectionist policies at home and open-market policies abroad. Section 301 and Section 337 still comprised the foundation of US trade policy, particularly in the area of trade-related IPR. In fact, they formed the base of the US response to major trade-related IPR conflicts with both China and South Africa during the 1990s.

Conclusion

The results of Congress' solution to the trade-based IPR problem have not been as fruitful as expected. Countries negotiated agreements with the US, but generally have not followed through to the full satisfaction of the US. IPR-dependent industries adopted policies that used the US government in the toughest cases where IPR protection was not forthcoming while at the same time helping cooperative countries police piracy. The combination of these policies brought the IPR issue to the headlines in the US and gave industry more effective avenues for protecting their IP. While the long-term success of US "aggressive unilateralism" has been mixed, its reception overseas has been decidedly hostile. During the 1990s, US trade policy centered on Section 301 provisions brought the US to the precipice of major trade wars with China and to the apex of public embarrassment in its IPR conflict with South Africa. Both cases clearly illustrate the problems developing countries have confronted with IPR in the changing dynamics of global competition.

Chapter Five

The Scramble for China

Introduction

China's emergence from isolation in the late 1970s and early 1980s opened significant investment and trade opportunities to Western interests. However, China's centrally planned economy, layers of bureaucracy, and rampant corruption proved to be formidable challenges in opening China's consumer markets. At the same time, China had embarked on a path of economic development, focusing on scientific and technological advancements that would place it on par with Western states early in the new millennium. Because of internal political turmoil, China had significant ground to cover in meeting its goal of technological progress. China's internal politics and the legacy of its cultural heritage (which does not recognize private property) posed significant challenges to demands for protecting foreign IPR.

The argument in this chapter centers on the development of IPR protection in emerging market economies. Several characteristics of these states are important in explaining the role and development of IPR protection in their markets. Economic development itself creates pressure for states to give industries inexpensive access to technology. As noted previously, one of the least expensive methods for acquiring technology is through IPR theft or piracy. Domestic IPR-dependent interests that would support the imposition of a strong IPR regime in the emerging market may be either weak or non-existent. The greatest pressure for strong IPR protection emanates from foreign interests, which seek to protect their trade and investments in the emerging market. In response, these developing states typically resist imposing stricter IPR regimes.

Internally, China showed little development of IPR-dependent interest groups that would support a strong IPR regime. China's domestic economic advances made it attractive to foreign trade and investment. In fact, much of China's economic progress through the 1980s and 1990s has been driven by contact with its trading partners, with foreign investment and trade propelling one of the fastest growing economies in the world. But China's attraction as a trade and investment partner has brought with it unwanted attention to its relatively weak foreign IPR protection policies.

China experienced two periods in its history when IPR proved to be an important factor in its development and in its relationships with foreign governments. What both periods had in common was that *foreign* interests were the driving force behind the move toward stronger IPR protection. China's first experience with IPR during the late 19th century was not fruitful. Foreign contacts and investors interested in protecting their market share in China forced the Chinese government to impose stronger IPR protection for foreign products. However, since no strong domestic sources of IPR support had emerged, China resisted the outside influence in its legal system. China's second encounter with IPR has been different in that it has been also accompanied by high rates of economic growth and a strong reliance on foreign investment and trade. These factors have made China's continued resistance to stronger IPR protection more difficult to orchestrate than in its first IPR experience.

China's Ancient Experience with IP

China's initial experience with IPR affairs can be traced to ancient times. Evidence dating prior to the Zhou dynasty in 1122 BCE has shown that authorities expressed concern with commodity identification.[1] In the Qin era, concern for the distribution of written materials appeared. Substantial efforts to regulate publication occurred with the rise of printing in the Tang period. In 835 AD, the Wenzong emperor issued an edict prohibiting the unauthorized republication of calendars, almanacs and other items. Official documents and histories were included in the edict just prior to the collapse of the Tang dynasty.While these concerns were present in ancient China, there was no indication that IPR existed in China (Alford 1995: 16-17). Much like Europe's experience with IPR, China's efforts to provide property rights to producers were not out of economic considerations; rather, they were an effort to strengthen imperial power. In this sense, the ban on reproduction of marks or other works was an effort to restrict material that ran counter to the imperial orthodoxy. Chinese culture generally militated against intellectual achievements being deemed private property. The Chinese considered past knowledge important for teaching moral lessons and other achievements, which mandated access to the common heritage of all Chinese people. Coupled with the need of elders to teach juniors through control and discipline, these cultural elements demanded the wide availability of China's intellectual heritage. Foreign intervention in the 18th century, however, would challenge these strong cultural influences.

Early Foreign Intervention in China

The first encounters between Western powers and Chinese civilization were tenuous, given that Chinese authorities openly discouraged contact with the West. The *waiyi* or "outer barbarians" were unwanted intruders. The government attempted to limit the *waiyi* influence by isolating their economic activities to the Canton (modern Guangzhou) and Macao areas in southeastern China. But by the 19th century, growing European impatience with the perceived inequity of the Chinese trade system and China's disinterest in Western products propelled European merchants to sell opium in China illegally. Eventually, China's balance of trade with the British and other Western powers went negative. Attempts to stop the opium trade were met with severe consequences. In the Opium War (1839-1842), the British forced open the interior of China and demanded concessions for British citizens in the Chinese legal system. Other states also sought this "most favored nation" status for Chinese trade. The expansion of trade brought with it ensuing complaints from Western merchants about the weak protection of IP.

Sporadic reports appeared of British trade names being used to sell opium and inferior grades of tea. But real attention to the IP problem did not emerge until the late 19th century during an unprecedented period of international concern for IPR. With the signing of the Paris convention for the Protection of Industrial Property (1883) and the Berne Convention for the Protection of Copyrights (1886), traders in China expected to receive protection for their products, even though China was not a party to the conventions. The Chinese had neither the experience with IP law nor the institutions to appropriately deal with IP issues. Soon, merchants lost any hope of receiving protection from the Chinese government and negotiated for protection with local representatives or consulates in China. But these actions had little impact because there was no way to enforce the agreements.

Following the Chinese government's failure to oust foreign influence in the fourth Boxer War of 1900, the British attempted to negotiate commercial treaties with China. This period was the era of financial imperialism, when Western powers competed for influence in China and made exploitative demands on the Chinese government. The Western powers expanded their negotiation to establish a complete commercial environment for their respective merchants. Having little room to maneuver, the Chinese signed a number of treaties with the British, including the Mackay Treaty of 1902, which provided for the protection of foreign trademarks in China (Alford 1995: 37). A similar treaty was signed with the United States in 1903.

But the implementation of the treaty's provisions failed, with the US and other countries claiming that the Chinese did not understand IP laws. While this may have been true, it differed little from the initial Western experience with IP. In the West IPR were a reward for bringing new ideas and inventions to the kingdom or state regardless of who actually invented or created the product first. This scenario also played out in China, where agencies gave patents for imitation of Western technology rather than for new ideas (Alford 1995: 46). Despite this, the Chinese understood the benefits that IPR protection could provide. Following the treaty signings, China made an attempt to codify IPR protection on a number of occasions.

In 1904 the government enacted trademark protection with the Trial Regulations for Trademark Registration. In 1910 the government also enacted the *Da Quing* Copyright Law. However, China's attempt to relegate foreign trademark and copyright holders to a secondary status next to Chinese nationals led to the laws' eventual collapse under foreign pressure. Attempts to revise the trademark law in 1923 and

1931 failed and a later version of the *Da Quing* Copyright Law also failed under the same pressure (Endeshaw 1996: 310).

Though the Western powers made substantial efforts to improve the protection of IPR in China, their diplomatic methods proved to be flawed. Hindered by self-serving foreign advisors, the West dismissed the help of domestic IP holders who could have given credible support to enacting tougher legislation (Alford 1995: 49). While treaties guaranteeing the protection of IP were signed, the West failed to uphold its promise to relinquish privileges that had been granted under previous Chinese governments. China's initial willingness to cooperate soon diminished. What the historical evidence demonstrates, however, is that China's original decision to implement an IPR protection policy was due specifically to foreign influence and pressure, not domestic economic concerns.

Internal struggles that transformed China from an imperial power to a warlord state interrupted the government's ability to translate the perceived benefits of IP into reality. Following consolidation of power by the Kuomintang in 1928, one of the first orders of business was to pass a new copyright law. The law protected moral and economic rights for Chinese productions over a thirty-year period; foreign works were protected for only ten years. While the government sought to promote trade with the law, the more important use for the law was a continuation of the political use of IPR. Registration was through the Ministry of Internal Affairs and works that ran counter to Kuomintang doctrine or other laws were not given protection. With the onset of World War II, the government imposed greater restrictions with mandatory reviews for material that ran counter to the Kuomintang or the philosophy of Sun Yat-sen.

In 1932, the government enacted new patent laws that protected both Chinese and foreign works. The implementation of these new laws, however, was not graceful. Not only did the laws presume a legal culture that did not exist, but, as with the enforcement of any law, they also presumed an institutional capacity for implementation. In fact, China did not have the legal experience or the technical knowledge to carry out an appropriate review of many patent applications. Moreover, with China's burgeoning population, the judicial system was inadequate to deal with the influx of legal cases. Even at the local level, mechanisms for dispute resolution such as trade associations or chambers of commerce could not be organized by the weak central government (Alford 1995: 48).

Ending Foreign Influence: The Rise of Communist China

The Kuomintang's short-lived reign ended in 1949 with its overthrow by Mao Zedong's Communist revolution. After assuming power, the Chinese communists repealed all laws passed by the Kuomintang. With its close ties to the Soviet Union, the ruling Chinese Communist Party adopted the Soviet model of IPR protection, which also reflected traditional Chinese thought on IPR. These ideas were rooted in the notion of bettering society through the accumulation and dispersion of knowledge. Hence, as a result of both ideological and cultural influences, the new communist government implemented an IPR regime based heavily on the notion that individual accomplishments were owned by all of society (Willard 1996: 417).

In this vein, the Chinese established a two-track system for protecting IP, passing two laws, the Provisional Regulations on the Protection of the Invention Right and the Patent Right of August 11, 1950 and the Provisional Regulations on Awards for Inventions, Technical Improvement, and Rationalization Proposals Relating to Production of May 6, 1954. The inventors received certificates of authorship and a monetary reward that replaced the monopoly privilege usually accorded inventions in patent systems. Most inventions issued certificates of authorship by the government were deemed critical to national security, which then gave the state control of the invention. Other inventions deemed less vital were issued patents vesting full control to the inventor with rights to royalties (Alford 1995: 57). No comparable copyright system was employed. This system marked the end of Western influence in Chinese IPR policy. China's purpose for developing the new IPR system was to promote economic development and to rid itself of centuries of foreign influence. Despite the incentives, the new IPR system produced little success. Piracy of foreign IP was on the rise with state agencies even engaging in the practice (Alford 1995: 61).

In the early 1960s China underwent significant political turmoil that would have a profound impact not just on IPR policy, but on China's long-term economic development. The central focus of the turmoil was revisionism. Internally, the Chinese Communist Party confronted the problem of rhetoric versus results. Some leaders grew weary of Mao's romantic vision of communist society, believing it only hindered real economic progress. As calls from Mao for new "socialist education" fell on deaf ears, his heavily indoctrinated army provided the base from which Mao launched "The Great Proletarian Cultural Revolution," which was more accurately described as a second revolution to create a property-less class (Fairbanks et al. 1978: 931).

Mao moved to eliminate those who opposed his cultural movement. He relied on the Chinese People's Liberation Army to force his agenda forward. Party power-holders were attacked and replaced, shattering the traditional party structure and replacing it with "revolutionary committees" comprised of army members and former party officials who had been "properly" indoctrinated. The end result was to give more civil power to the army's personnel, who were given high-level administrative positions. Of course, the drive to create the property-less society had an impact at all levels of society and particularly on the elite classes.

Universities closed while faculty and other elites were transferred to farms in order to study and to gain experience with manual labor. The political upheaval prompted reforms that brought into doubt the appropriateness of material rewards for scientists and other inventors. Academics were singled out for putting their careers and professional development ahead of the Communist Party's goals (Alford 1995: 63-65). Consequently, the State Council adopted new "Regulations on Awards for Inventions," which stated that "[a]ll inventions are the property of the state, and no person...may claim a monopoly over them..." (Willard 1996: 418). Patents were ideologically unacceptable and no longer available. Despite the rhetoric of the era, the government still recognized the need to advance science and technology. The emphasis was no longer on honorary and material rewards, however, as the government sought to enforce its ideological-political rhetoric (Subcommittee on US Trade with China 1984: 20). Clearly, the Chinese did not want to give up incentives to produce technologically valuable products. However, the reconciliation of such incentives with the property-less class society was difficult. IPR protection was cut back significantly, but the long-term effects of the Cultural Revolution would be felt mostly in terms of China's desire for scientific and technological progress.

Recovering from the Revolution: The Post-Mao Period

Mao and the "Gang of Four" (protagonist members of the Central Committee, including Mao's wife, who advocated the harshest reforms during the revolution) looked to the masses instead of an elite core of qualified people to advance China's technological progress. But what this produced was the dismantling of an infrastructure that had been built up over the previous decade (Simon 1989: 600). Chinese science and technology stagnated while Western states surpassed China in terms of scientific gains. While the West was about to undergo the computer and information revolution, an ideological tug-of-war slowed China's progress and threatened to disintegrate completely its scientific potential. The damage that the Cultural Revolution inflicted on China's technological progress and infrastructure was more than had been initially estimated. Not only was China's progress damaged, but its ability to escape foreign reliance on technology was also seriously crippled.

The end of the Cultural Revolution in the mid-1970s brought about another reevaluation of China's IPR laws. The drive to change China's patent laws was the result of a long political struggle that began in 1976. Chinese Communist Party Chairman Hua Guofeng announced the "Four Modernizations" plan. The plan's goals were to attain modernization in agriculture, industry, national defense, and science and technology by the year 2000, while in the process overtaking many of the developed countries in these areas (Townsend and Womack 1986: 142). To accomplish this monumental task, the government placed the acquisition of technology at the forefront of the agenda. Trade, foreign direct investment, and domestic research would be a priority in the "Four Modernizations." But Hua would not be around to see this plan through, as he was ousted by the increasingly popular Deng Xiaoping.

After Deng assumed China's leadership, he purged Hua's supporters from the Chinese leadership, at the 1980 Third Plenum of the Central Committee, and replaced Hua's grandiose scheme with an approach that embraced a readiness to do anything necessary to modernize China. For example, in 1984 price controls were loosened and enterprise autonomy in the industrial/urban sectors was increased. Restrictions on foreign direct investment were also eased (Townsend and Womack 1986: 149). The introduction of these reforms should be noted in the larger context of what amounts to a reorganization of China's entire governmental structure. The process included the enactment of thousands of new laws across the country and the restructuring of administrative bureaus to deal with new legal cases, which the government encouraged (Schlesinger 1995: 98).

During this process, Deng concluded that inventors needed incentives to produce but that these same inventors had to fulfill their obligations to the state. Despite Deng's support, internal opposition to IPR reform mounted. Some opponents were concerned about the potential of Western corporations to dominate the Chinese markets while others pointed to potential economic problems in using foreign reserves to pay royalties. Deng nevertheless pressed for reform and achieved it with changes to China's constitution, the accession of China to the World Intellectual Property Rights Organization in 1980, the establishment of a Patent Bureau in 1980, and the passage of the 1984 Patent Law. The 1984 Patent Law was the product of extensive research by the Chinese. Legal experts visited over thirty different countries and solicited the comments of Chinese citizens from various regions (Zheng 1987: 349). The implementation of the law, however, was not as carefully planned. Again the impact of the Cultural Revolution was felt. An "education gap" had formed as a result of China's youth being involved in the revolution while schools and universities were shut down (Special Subcommittee on United States Trade with China 1984: 35).

The end result for Deng's plan was an opening of China's consumer market to the world. China's trade figures clearly illustrate this point. Prior to 1980, China was a mere statistical hiccup in international trade figures. During the 1980s, China's trade figures show dramatic growth. Following the post-Mao transition period around 1980, imports and exports increased at a faster rate than in the Mao period. Imports and exports have grown in tandem, indicating a growth in export production and the consumption of foreign goods. China's trade with Western countries contributed to this growth. The US and Japan were the primary beneficiaries of China's post-Mao open economy reforms, with Chinese imports from these two countries growing substantially after 1980. China itself has also benefited as exports to the West dramatically increased.

Despite China's growing trade relationship, investors were still weary of sinking billions of dollars into a socialist, centrally-planned economy. Though China relied on trade as a major part of its economic strategy, its turn to foreign investment represented the biggest break with its stringent isolationist past (Riskin 1995: 325). The government created special economic zones with favorable tax rates, profit repatriation and other special provisions in the hope of attracting investment from overseas. More than forty special laws or decrees were enacted for foreign investors (Riskin 1995: 325). The result of these overtures is clearly illustrated in Figure 5.1, as foreign direct investment increased dramatically in the 1980s and through the first half of the 1990s.

Figure 5:1 Net Foreign Direct Investment in China, 1980-1994

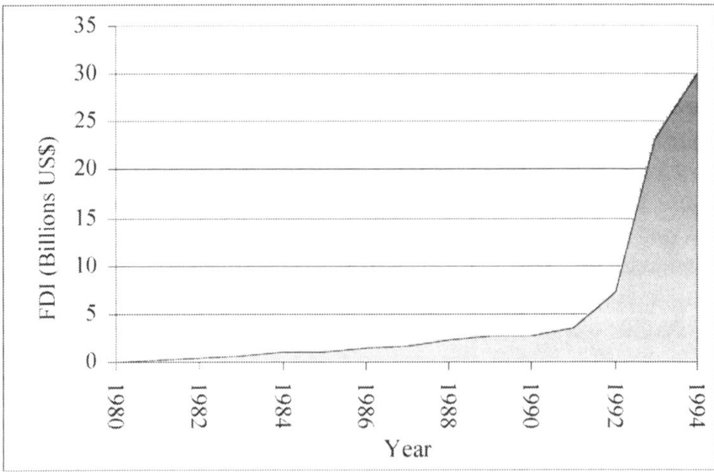

Source: *World Bank*

After 1990, investor confidence in the Chinese government and its policies grew substantially. Investors poured money into China with the hope of capturing hefty portions of the world's largest untapped consumer market. Investors' home governments provided strong support in protecting investment assets in China. Some of the protective actions were targeted at IPR protection. China had placed itself on a path toward greater economic growth and development, setting the stage for its second experience with foreign intervention on the IPR issue.

Sino-American Trade-Related IPR Affairs

Reforms to China's IPR regime began with improved relations with the United States. In 1979, the US and China signed the "Agreement on Trade Relations," which provided that "[E]ach Party shall seek, under its laws and with due regard to international practice, to ensure to legal or natural persons of the other Party protection of patents and trademarks equivalent to the patent and trademark protection correspondingly accorded by the other Party" (Endeshaw 1996: 311). The agreement addressed copyright laws, with the Chinese government promising to provide copyright protection to US nationals.

China's economic and political reforms quickly caught the attention of lawmakers in the US. In early 1983 members of the House Committee on Energy and Commerce traveled to China to assess the economic changes and their impact on China's relationship with the US. The Committee's report reflects the perceived gains from expanded trade with China, but it also pointed out what might be considered "growing pains" in the relationship. As noted earlier, China's post-revolution economic strategy was driven toward domestic economic development. That goal did not change in the Deng era, but the means of achieving it were definitely altered from the early post-revolution days.

China's domestic development was to be divided into two sectors, the rural and the urban (House Committee on Energy and Commerce 1983: 6). In the rural sector, the government still required peasants to produce some products for distribution by the state at low prices, but any surplus could be sold at market prices by the peasants (subject to taxation). The long-term goal for the rural sector was self-sufficiency. The urban sector plan was the most ambitious. The government's primary goal for the urban sector was to modernize the infrastructure in order to compete with developed countries. While industrial growth had been based predominantly on heavy industry, the Chinese leadership expressed a desire to move away from such growth patterns and to promote a light-industry-based economy. Technology transfers and knowledge would be needed and trade and investment were the quickest vehicles to attain this. The leadership also concluded that the relationship with the US would be crucial to achieving these goals.

As the Committee report points out, in any relationship, the Chinese judge the value of the relationship based on mutual benefits.

To the Committee, this meant that the Chinese would not tolerate large trade deficits or any other type of detrimental byproduct of the evolving trade relationship. But closing the gaps and improving the relationship would not be so easy. The US was still fixated on the Cold War view of China as a communist state. Technology transfers between the two countries underwent intense scrutiny by national security agencies and defense experts checking for "dual use" technology. Similar concerns also retarded the approval of trade licenses. Thus, American bureaucracy would be an obstacle to improving trade relations with China (House Committee on Energy and Commerce 1983: 7-8). The Chinese reaction to these issues was to express concern to the Committee about the status of the Sino-American relationship.

Other political considerations hampered trade progress as well. Social activists often targeted China's human rights policies as reason for stripping its most-favored-nation status. US lawmakers debated increased trade contact with China in the shadow of concern for Taiwan's security and China's intentions toward Taiwan. In the early 1980s additional concern over China's desire to reacquire Hong Kong, a major financial and capital market of the world, caused deep apprehension in Washington. While these have been long-standing concerns for US administrations, Chinese domestic barriers to trade also became contentious issues for discussion. The House Committee brought several matters of contention to the leadership's attention; among the issues were price discrimination against foreign firms providing Chinese goods and services, the lack of office space for foreign firms in major cities, the restrictions on US scholars studying in China, and the level of patent protection for US goods exported to China. While the Chinese promised to address most of the issues, the patent problems would really test the strength of the Sino-American trade relationship.

China's growing economic relationship with the US proved to be the catalyst for shaping China's current IPR policy. Growing global trade relations meant increased competition that forced the US government to actively pursue protection for its primary trade comparative advantage, namely IP. China, on the other hand, was expanding its economic capabilities and needed to acquire technology in the most cost-efficient manner possible. But at the same time, China's decision to enter into the world markets was the catalyst for its IPR system. Foreign interests again pressured the Chinese for protection. The US decision to protect its industrial IP overseas and China's decision to enter the world markets set the stage for the emergence of IP piracy as a central theme in Sino-American trade relations.

US corporations enlisted the aid of the United States government, claiming significant losses in the Chinese market. For instance, Parker Brothers claimed that the piracy of its popular board game "Monopoly" caused US$200 million in losses. Levi Strauss claimed that China illegally produced and exported 1.2 million pairs of its jeans. Oranges pulled from garbage cans were stamped with the Sunkist trademark and sold in Chinese markets (Ramjerdi and D'amato 1995: 181). The piracy of computer software grew increasingly troublesome to United States corporations as well. The source of these problems seemed to be in China's weak IPR laws. USTR Carla Hills addressed this issue with the Chinese. Despite reforms in IPR protection brought about by the early 1980 laws, major flaws still existed in protecting IPR in China. The 1984 Patent Law excluded chemicals and pharmaceuticals, and it did not affect current inventions, models or designs for which patent applications had been filed before October 1984. Computer software was also left unprotected in China.

The Sino-American IPR Conflict Take One: the Laws

The gaps in China's IP laws drew repeated calls from the US for the Chinese government to improve protection. With the passage of the 1988 Omnibus Trade and Competitiveness Act in the United States, the USTR possessed the bilateral tools to pressure China on the IPR issue. In 1989, the USTR placed China on the priority watch list and warned the government that reform would be needed in their IPR regime. In 1990, China passed a new copyright law to address some of the foreign concerns over copyright protection. The groundwork for this law was established with the 1982 Constitution and China's 1986 Civil Law, which gave citizens the rights to authorship. Though the changes were a step in the right direction, they fell far short of US expectations.

The law itself was not in compliance with the Berne Convention and the Universal Copyright Convention, the primary global agreements for the protection of copyrighted works. Chinese authors were protected whether they published in the country or outside it, but foreign authors had no protection unless the work was published in

China. This provision left the floodgates open to piracy, particularly of computer software, which is traditionally covered under copyright laws (Willard 1996: 423-424).

The US was not satisfied with China's progress toward adopting all the necessary laws to protect IPR. Exporters estimated losses to China's pirates of US$10-25 million in sales in 1987 and computer software piracy losses of US$70-150 million each year (Endeshaw 1996: 312). In 1991, the USTR changed China's trade status to a priority foreign country and initiated a Special 301 investigation into China's IPR protection. By December of 1991, the clouds of a trade war loomed overhead. In the final hours before the US government was to impose trade sanctions, China signed a Memorandum of Understanding (MOU) that addressed US concerns over China's IPR laws. In the MOU, China *promised* significant reforms to its copyright, patent and trademark laws. As a result, the US withdrew its Special 301 investigation and placed China on the watch list in April 1992. The US proclaimed the agreement as the most successful Special 301 investigation to date (Chien-Hale 1997: 217).

Reaction to the MOU was cautious but optimistic. China managed to keep the United States IPR issue under control, allowing its trade surplus with the United States to grow quickly. But as Rosen and Husijian point out, there was a big difference between the *laws* that were on the books and the actual *enforcement* of them. Bootleg videos, CDs, music tapes, and movies appeared on Chinese street corners even before they were officially released in the United States. Microsoft, Sun Microsystems and other computer companies found their programs pirated in China. Chrysler also mysteriously found its Jeep Cherokee being produced three miles from its own Chinese manufacturing facility (Rosen and Husisian 1995: 56). Many US corporations argued that China encouraged this behavior and that some Chinese officials actually owned stakes in some of the pirating factories (Rosen and Husisian 1995: 56). As a result, the corporations concluded that China had reneged on its 1992 MOU with the United States.

The sentiments of the corporations appeared to be correct. As Table 5:1 shows, China's IPR law and protection scores (derived from the methodology in chapter two) did not budge. Patent protection scores remained the same across all three time periods as well as copyright and trademark scores. These scores indicate that China had considerable room for improvement in their IPR protection policies.

Moreover, the scores indicate that China did not follow through on promises to improve its protection policies, much to the frustration of foreign corporations. These data reveal that the most interesting aspect of China's IPR regime is where the weakness lies. All the law scores indicate that China's laws do provide moderate to high levels of protection for IPR. However, the enforcement of those laws creates a vacuum in IPR protection. The government adopted a strategy of legislatively appeasing foreign pressures but being lax in the actual enforcement. However, even with this IPR problem, the government's policies have not deterred investment. As Figure 5:1 indicates, the amount of investment in China through 1994 actually *increased* substantially. Given the potential size of the Chinese consumer market, investors were willing to sacrifice some level of protection for the huge investment returns in the large consumer market.

Table 5:1 China's IPR Law and Protection Scores

Category	1988	1991	1994
Patent Laws	3	3	3
Copyright Laws	6	6	6
Trademark Laws	8	8	8
Patent Protection	6	6	6
Copyright Protection	16	16	16
Trademark Protection	12	12	12

The Sino-American IPR Conflict Take Two: Enforcement

The enforcement issue took center stage in Sino-American trade-related IPR. While this problem seemed straightforward to the United States, the sources of China's enforcement problems were and still are much more complex. Willard (1996) cited several reasons for China's enforcement problems. First, there is a lack of traditional respect for IPR in China. Part of this has been discussed previously with reference to China's cultural heritage. A related issue is the lack of public awareness of IP issues (Willard 1996: 428). The concepts created by IPR legislation are "peculiar" to judges, lawyers, and citizens. Willard concluded that *domestic involvement in the IP system is low and will most likely remain low until China moves closer to a market economy and economic incentives to protect IP increase.* What Willard suggests is an evolutionary progress to the development of an IPR culture and institutions that are capable of dealing with complex IP issues. China's long-standing cultural practices cannot change to Western standards without going through periods of adaptation and adjustment.

Regional differences within China also contributed to enforcement problems. Localized trade wars erupted in some provinces, indicating authorities were more concerned with developing their local economies than they were with participating in a national economy (Willard 1996: 428-429). Central enforcement mechanisms were hampered and set back by military and government cadres that owned a stake in pirating operations. Provincial and military leaders have been reluctant to move against pirates. Even if they do move against pirates, they ultimately faced the third problem Willard cites, namely an inadequate judiciary.

The whole court system is generally ill-prepared to deal with the IPR issue. Many courts have been understaffed while courts and lawyers are generally inexperienced in the interpretation of IPR law. Judges have virtually no experience with these types of laws and lack the necessary background to rule on these cases (Willard 1996: 430-31). Though the government established special courts to deal with IPR issues specifically, the efficiency of the courts did not improve. Of particular importance to foreign IP holders was the problem that foreign lawyers could not litigate in Chinese courts. All court business had to be conducted by Chinese counsel, which hindered foreign IP cases by creating time delays and extra expenses.

The enforcement issue resulted in additional losses for US corporations doing business in China. The US government argued that China's failure to protect IPR was a significant market access barrier and that the lack of protection widened the trade gap between the two countries. The latter concern was most important from China's perspective because of mounting domestic pressure in the US to close the trade deficit with China. After seeing no significant response from the Chinese, USTR Mickey Kantor again designated China a "priority foreign country" and instigated a Special 301 investigation into China's IPR protection practices. The move upset Chinese officials, who had just completed reforming China's property rights regime (Chien-Hale 1997: 218). China's official news agency, *Xinhua*, reported that Washington had again meddled in China's domestic affairs by calling for changes to its judicial system and laws. Chinese officials argued that demands by the US to allow wholly foreign-funded press, publication, audio, and video enterprises were beyond the scope of IPR protection (Chien-Hale 1997: 218). Negotiations to resolve the differences ensued and but rapidly failed. Kantor announced US$1.08 billion in trade sanctions to be imposed if agreement could not be reached. China likewise announced its own set of retaliatory trade sanctions.

The US government was concerned not only with the financial losses two of its major economic sectors were suffering (the entertainment and high tech industries), but also with solidifying market share for American corporations operating in China. Despite teetering on the brink of a major trade war, the United States and China signed thirty-four new contracts worth US$6 billion in Beijing and another eight contracts worth US$2 billion in Shanghai. The contracts were in the areas of energy efficiency, technology development, nuclear fuel research, renewable energy, electricity, gas and oil, all of which rely to some degree on IPR protection (Endeshaw 1996: 317). The US government actively pressured China not to sign similar contracts with other countries in some of these areas. The new contracts proved significant, but the threatened trade war illustrated the importance of holding market share in China.

Had the trade war erupted, one potential US loss was with the Boeing Corporation. China threatened to cancel an order for Boeing's new 777 passenger jets and to give the contract to its only significant competitor, the European Consortium Airbus. Boeing would have lost its sixty-percent share of China's aerospace industry, which was not developed enough to make IPR piracy a threat to Boeing. Thus, Boeing had no stake in the IPR trade war that loomed on the horizon. As Endeshaw argued, China managed to pit two major sectors of the American economy against each other: the entertainment and high tech sectors against the aerospace industry (1996: 319). Chinese authorities exploited this divide in US industries by threatening sanctions against US non-IPR dependent industries.

The Chinese government, however, also understood the benefits derived from the US trade relationship. China still sought investment and technology from the US. The second IPR protection dispute went well beyond established deadlines, but eventually an agreement was negotiated by the two sides. The MOU included major provisions that called for:

Raids on pirate factories and the destruction of piracy equipment
A nine-month "special enforcement period" during which counterfeiters would be rooted out
Tougher penalties for piracy
Enhanced customs inspections at China's borders
A halt to counterfeit good exports from China
Transparency of censorship rules and more access to the enforcement system
The lifting of all import restrictions on US products
The submission of regular reports to the US by China on the state of IPR enforcement (Endeshaw 1996: 325-326)

The reaction to the 1995 MOU was mixed. Some industry leaders suggested that pirates will always be one step ahead of the enforcement efforts because they are so well connected to the Chinese leadership. Others questioned whether the leadership had the power or the will to carry out the agreement (Endeshaw 1996: 326). But questions of the leadership's willingness to carry out such a campaign were quickly addressed.

The Chinese government in the following year stepped up enforcement practices, cracking down on pirates in several highly publicized raids:

> Hunan Province: January through May of 1996— the government conducted 3,201 inspections for copyright, patent and trademark infringement. 89,500 pirated tapes, 14,800 pirated CDs, and 97,418 pirated books were seized. Training classes were held for 23,900 leading and management cadres, enhancing awareness of the IP issue (Foreign Broadcast Information Service, July 19, 1996)
>
> Hangzhou Province, June 1996— government raids confiscated pirated CDs, videos, audio tapes, and laser discs. Trademark proceedings against "Mitsubishi Cold Storage and Air Conditioning Service Department" were instituted for the improper use of the Mitsubishi Corporation's trademark name (Foreign Broadcast Information Service, July 19, 1996).

> Guangzhou Province, June 1996— government crack-down on copyright infringement with tighter border patrols. 45,000 raids on pirating facilities, including production houses, warehouses and retail outlets, were carried out with 1.9 million pirated audio and visual products confiscated (Foreign Broadcast Information Service, July 19, 1996).

While the raids could be interpreted as a mere show for the US government, they were nonetheless impressive for their speed and scope. Despite their efforts, the Chinese still pressed their case about the manner in which the US addressed the IPR issue and the general way in which the US conducted its trade relations with China. In a blistering *Xinhua* commentary, the Chinese government attacked US trade policies, particularly Section 301, advocating an international uprising against unfair US trade practices:

> In the past two years, trade frictions between the United States and various countries have continued, and the extent of the areas involved was much larger than in the past ...trade disputes have arisen ... [because] the United States starts most of the trade disputes and because of other intrinsic factors. First it is its willful and obstinate "unilateral action"...What most embodies the US "unilateral" trade policy is the US Trade Act's "Special 301" and "Super 301" Clauses ...Second it is a very naked double standard. The United States practices double standards in the areas of human rights, democracy, environmental protection, and arms embargoes. It is the same in trade ...Third it is power trade and economic hegemonism. The US economic blockade of Cuba ...sanctions against Iran and other countries ... [show] that the United States is attempting to practice its already outdated extraterritoriality. This not only runs counter to the principle of free trade in the world and harms the interests of various countries, but also harms the credibility of US trade policy (Foreign Broadcast Information Service, July 26, 1996).

So, while China conceded to US demands, it was less than content with the methods used in the process. US "aggressive unilateralism" had brought another country into compliance with US trade demands, while bringing both countries to the brink of a major trade war twice. Nonetheless, the US achieved its trade objectives, forcing China to comply with US IPR standards.

Conclusion

China presented a prime example of a country in major economic and political transformation. Early in China's history, there was no formalized practice of IPR protection, with concern for IPR only accorded to enhance or sustain imperial power. With the introduction of foreign interests to China, IPR became more important to foreign commercial interests. The Chinese government came under increasing pressure to adopt a system of laws with which it had no prior experience. The implementation of an IPR regime brought to China the Western conception of IPR law. As there was minimal domestic experience and a limited base of support in China for such a system, Western states found it difficult to get compliance with IPR protection rules. China's willingness to adopt and enforce such rules came about only when Western states pressured it to do so.

The Sino-American trade-related dispute in IPR protection highlighted several points. China had no interest in adopting a full IPR protection regime—both laws and enforcement practices—given its domestic economic development plans. While government corruption in the IP pirating business was prevalent, China understood the need to obtain inexpensive technology as rapidly as possible if it was to become an economic force in the global markets. However, the interests driving the adoption of the domestic IPR regime had a foreign source, not a domestic one. China was yet to develop the technological capacity and the interest group institutions that would spawn domestic pressures for increased IPR protection. Foreign interests have been most successful using economic leverage to force the Chinese into protecting IPR. At the same time, China also demonstrated its willingness to retaliate against US "aggressive unilateralism," in part because it had the capacity to do so. US industry wanted its share of China's consumer market as much as China wanted US technology. China strategically pitted major US industrial sectors against each other because of the interests many sectors had in the Chinese market. China's economic power in this instance gave it considerable economic leverage against the US—a luxury few countries possess.

Chapter Six

Life, Death and Intellectual Property: The South Africa-US Patent Dispute*

Introduction

In the era of globalization, trade disputes often pit the economic interests of developed countries against the social and economic interests of developing countries. One such example involves trade relations between South Africa and the United States. In the early 1990s, the South African government came under pressure from the Clinton Administration to adjust its domestic patent laws to continue pharmaceutical patent protection. The disagreement between South Africa and the United States centered on changes to the Medicines and Related Substances Control Act, which allowed the Health Minister to abolish patent rights for pharmaceuticals, to issue compulsory licenses, and to allow parallel imports of pharmaceuticals with the goal being to lower pharmaceutical prices. The US government wanted the offending clauses repealed, guaranteeing full protection to foreign pharmaceutical patents. However, the South African government maintained that it needed these tools to combat problems in its healthcare system, including the burdens inflicted by the HIV/AIDS crisis. Because of the patent issue, the US removed privileges for South Africa under the generalized system of preferences (GSP) and moved to impose harsher economic sanctions.

The argument in this chapter draws from material presented in the previous five chapters. While the South Africa-US patent dispute ostensibly represents another Section 301 case for US corporate interests, the essence of the dispute is grounded solidly in the issues raised in chapter one. The dispute is representative of the IPR protection issues trading states face when they are at different development levels. The dilemma the South African government faced was one of property rights versus subsistence rights—the protection of IPR for pharmaceuticals versus the need for pharmaceuticals in order to combat the HIV/AIDS epidemic. At stake for US corporations was monopoly power and market share in South Africa's pharmaceutical market; at stake for South Africans was something more important: life and death.

Problems in South Africa's Health Care System

In 1994 President Nelson Mandela's government faced at least two problems in health care. The first was the legacy of inequality in health care and treatment that emerged from the apartheid system's racially discriminatory practices. Approximately one-fifth of the population (predominantly white) enjoyed private health insurance and quality medical care while the remainder (predominantly black and colored) relied on racially segregated, inadequate public facilities (Benatar 1997: 1537). Racial segregation had been a primary force in creating a two-tier system where white populations with infectious diseases could both afford and receive treatment, while black populations with such diseases went without care or the health problems were simply legislated away from the view of the white population. No case illustrated this more than apartheid policies concerning tuberculosis (TB) infection.

Under the Nationalists' apartheid government, South Africa undertook a massive effort to stem the spread of TB in South Africa. Despite new treatments and a better understanding of how black South Africans were infected with TB,

> ...South African local and state authorities...relied primarily on legislative instruments to deal with the problem of TB among blacks. Using a long list of public health acts, urban areas acts, influx control laws, slum clearance acts, housing

> legislation, group areas acts and, ultimately acts establishing bantustans as "independent national states" beyond the boundaries of white South Africa, South African authorities ... methodically removed the health problems of blacks from the purview of white society (Packard 1989: 299).

Thus, reductions in TB cases post-1965 were not a product of better treatment or living conditions, but rather a decline in *reported* TB infections among the black and colored populations. These reporting failures resulted directly from the state's apartheid policies. The legacy of such policies was still reflected in 1994 when the TB notification rate for blacks was 180 per 100,000, whereas the notification rate for whites was 17 per 100,000 (World Bank estimates in Benatar 1997: 1538). Additional evidence of disparity can be found in infant mortality rates, maternal mortality rates and life expectancy figures (Benatar 1997).

The second problem Mandela's government faced was the Acquired Immune Deficiency Syndrome (AIDS) crisis and its subsequent impact on the health care system and the economy. South Africa's first two AIDS cases were reported in 1982, but by 1995, the number of cases had grown to 8784. The cases of human immunodeficiency virus (HIV) infection were thought to be much higher, with surveys showing that possibly 1.8 million people had been infected with the HIV (Jochelson 1999: 233). Studies at that time predicted that by the year 2000, approximately 3.7 to 4.1 million would be infected with the HIV (Jochelson 1999: 233). The most recent UNAIDS/WHO Report has placed the estimate of HIV infection at approximately 4.2 million South Africans, the largest population of HIV-infected people among all countries in sub-Saharan Africa. As a percentage of the total population, approximately twenty per cent of South Africa's population is infected, ranking it sixth in Africa behind Botswana, Swaziland, Zimbabwe, Lesotho, and Zambia. Additionally, the UNAIDS/WHO report estimated that South Africa's residual orphan problem has affected 420,000 children. Within South Africa, some provinces have experienced epidemics that are worse than the national average. According to government data released by the Ministry of Health, prevalence rates for some provinces have hovered around 30 per cent or higher.[1] In Kwazulu-Natal and Northwest provinces, infection rates among pregnant women (age 15-40) were

19.90 per cent and 25.13 per cent respectively (Swanevelder, Kustner, and Vanmiddelkoop 1998). The problem extends, however, beyond infection rates.

Through the late 1980s and 1990s, the subsequent problems associated with AIDS appeared in full force. Tuberculosis infections and mortality rates increased dramatically as AIDS patients became more susceptible to infection and disease with the weakening of their immune systems. From 1994 to 1995, TB mortality rates rose from 38 to 53 per 100,000 males and from 15 to 23 per 100,000 females, with the most incidents of death being recorded in provinces that had the highest incidence of HIV prevalence among women (Kwazulu-Natal and North West) (Kleinschmidt 1999). But the impact of the AIDS crisis extended far beyond healthcare to the whole South African economy.

Because the HIV is transmitted primarily through sexual activity, the greatest proportion of the population affected is between fifteen and forty years of age, essentially the active labor force. Among those people infected with the virus, death occurs six to twelve years after infection. In the long term, these data indicate that the size of South Africa's working-age population is expected to erode as HIV infections increase. Though the national effect is difficult to assess, it is expected that corporations could expect increasing payroll costs and decreased employee production in the future, while medical and life insurance rates could increase across the country (Nevin 1998).

Confronted by these conditions, Mandela's government moved to alleviate problems in the health care system. In April 1997, the government issued a White Paper (a policy objective briefing) for the Transformation of the Health System in South Africa. The paper outlined the government's objectives in increasing access to health services, ensuring access to pharmaceuticals and strengthening disease prevention and health promotion. In part, the goal was to alleviate the disparity in health care, particularly between the rural and urban sectors. In doing so, the government needed to address the high costs of pharmaceuticals in South Africa.

The Pharmaceuticals Issue

Pharmaceuticals in South Africa were priced above costs for the same drugs being sold in other countries in the region and in other parts of the world. Table 6:1 illustrates examples of the cost disparity.

Table 6:1 Sample of Drug Prices in Four Countries (ZAR)

Drug	South Africa	Zambia	New Zealand	Canada
Zantac	R424.47	R252.30	R100.08	R179.42
Tagamet	R364.61	R47.69	R100.10	R173.65
Prozac	R254.62	N/A	R194.66	R133.22
Losec	R387.41	R21.06	R216.70	R182.57

Source: Figures supplied by J H O Pretorius, Deputy Director General of Health Services in Kale 1995.

The data show that prices tended to be higher in South Africa than in other countries. Ironically, drugs exported from South Africa could cost less in the recipient country than in South Africa (Kale 1995: 2). Part of the blame for the higher prices lay with the South African distribution system. For instance, South Africa was one of only three countries in the world that levied a value added tax on pharmaceuticals. Despite this tax, pharmaceutical costs theoretically should have been mitigated because of the shorter distribution process where doctors often dispensed medicines directly without pharmacies or other retailers involved. Nevertheless, prices in South Africa remained high relative to other countries.

The Impact of AIDS

The AIDS crisis highlighted the drug pricing issue and the inequitable medical treatment in South Africa. Treatment regimens for HIV-infected individuals could cost upwards of US$10,000 a year (Ackiron 1991). The price for these drugs was well beyond the financial capacity of most South Africans. State funding for HIV treatment was the only recourse for many people. However, the cost of the treatments was too exorbitant, even for the government. In early 1999, South Africa's Health Minister Nkosazana Zuma removed state funding for a program to distribute the anti-viral drug Zidovudine (AZT) to pregnant

HIV-infected women, arguing that the scarce resources may be better allocated in prevention programs (Baleta 1999: 908).

The political fallout over the cost issue reached international levels, with potential boycotts of the July 2000 World AIDS Conference held in Durban, South Africa. Domestically, the Western Cape Province broke with national policy, supplying the drug as needed to pregnant women. Zuma later accused the Western Cape's New National Party of using AZT to buy votes in elections (Baleta 1999: 908). The indirect fallout from the AZT issue and more directly from the drug pricing problem as a whole was not limited to boycotts and allegations of impropriety. The South African government's solution to the pricing problem placed it on a collision course with the US government and multinational corporations.

Addressing the Pharmaceutical Pricing Problem

The government's response to the pharmaceutical pricing problem came in the form of the Medicines and Related Substances Control Amendment Act, submitted to Parliament in August 1997. Dr. Olive Shisana, Director General of Health, said that the bill reflected the Department of Health's "commitment to the delivery of affordable health care to the entire South African population...[as] high costs of medicines have been identified as one of the major reasons why ordinary consumers find it increasingly difficult to meet their medical bills" (Shisana 1997).

In practical terms, the bill sought to amend the 1965 Medicines and Related Substances Act in several ways. The bill would

- Establish a drug pricing committee
- Regulate the purchase and sale of medicines by wholesalers
- Provide procedures for expediting essential medicines
- Allow physicians to make generic drug substitutions
- Provide measures for the supply of more affordable medicines in certain circumstances

The last two measures proved to be the most controversial aspects of the bill. Section 15(c) of the bill gave the Health Minister extraordinary powers for increasing the conditions for the supply of affordable drugs, including abrogating patent rights to pharmaceuticals issued under South Africa's Patents Act of 1978 and the importation of identical pharmaceutical compounds from manufacturers other than the registered owner. The bill also allowed for generic substitutions, a common practice in many countries (National Assembly of South Africa 1997).

Before the legislature passed the bill, the US State Department had instructed US Ambassador James Joseph to express strong opposition to the pending changes in South Africa's pharmaceutical statutes. The bill passed despite testimony in Parliamentary hearings by US officials opposing it. After the bill's passage in November 1997, constitutional challenges by the South African Pharmaceuticals Industry (supported by European and American industry representatives) delayed its implementation. During the challenge period, the Ministry of Health introduced a bill that repealed the contentious elements of section 15(c); however, it reintroduced the provisions of section 15(c) after the public hearings were completed. In December 1998, President Mandela signed the bill into law much to the consternation of the South African Pharmaceutical Manufacturers Association and the Pharmaceutical Research and Manufacturers of America (PhRMA), both of which vehemently opposed the bill. For interest groups, the signing of the bill posed potentially global ramifications for IPR protection. In the US, the PhRMA contended that South Africa's action violated the TRIPS agreement and utilized Section 301 provisions in seeking the assistance of the US government to confront South Africa's government.

The United States' Motivation

In a letter sent to the Special Assistant to the Section 301 Committee, the PhRMA highlighted South Africa, contending that it had abandoned its obligations under the TRIPS agreement and had weakened IPR protection for pharmaceuticals. The letter also noted South Africa's recent statements at the WHO advocating a decrease in patent protection for pharmaceuticals. Subsequently, the PhRMA recommended that South Africa be added to the USTR's priority country list (Herzfeld 1999). In April 1998 and 1999, the USTR placed South Africa on the Special 301 Watch List, based partly on the new revisions to South Africa's pharmaceuticals law.

In making its decision, the USTR complained that the Medicines Act granted to the Health Minister "ill-defined authority to issue compulsory licenses, authorize parallel imports and potentially otherwise abrogate patent rights" (USTR 1999: 22). The USTR agreed with the PhRMA and viewed the law as being symptomatic of South Africa's leadership in the WHO in trying to reduce the level of protection for pharmaceuticals under the TRIPS agreement. Additionally, USTR Charlene Barshefsky made it clear that she intended to address the IPR issue with the South African government and to begin an investigation of South Africa's progress in addressing these concerns beginning in September 1999, with the possibility of moving South Africa to the priority watch list or the priority country list. Doing so would carry the possibility of sanctions against South Africa, though the likelihood of the latter action seemed remote, given stated opposition to sanctions by Clinton Administration officials.

Shortly after Barshefsky's report in 1999, the State Department, the USTR, and the Department of Commerce acted to withhold preferential treatment for South Africa under the GSP. The decision was reported in the South African media, but the government remained silent on the development. In the US, however, the political cost of the South African patent issue was high, particularly for Vice President Al Gore.

The Political Fallout

As co-chair of the primary US-South African trade commission with former Deputy President (now President) Thabo Mbeki, Gore was the administration's primary spokesperson on the patent issue. In that role, he was at the center of a multitude of political forces with significant interests in the dispute. US law mandated one such force, requiring the USTR to engage South Africa's government in negotiations to restructure its statutes to protect US IP overseas. As Vice President, Gore was constitutionally obligated to uphold and to execute such laws. However, as is often the case in trade issues, political interests had significant influence in how the laws were enforced. The pharmaceutical industry and members of Congress supported the effort to change South Africa's law, giving both the Congress and the Vice President a *financial* interest in seeing that the law was carried out.

According to the Center for Responsive Politics, the pharmaceutical and health care industry contributed US$71,500 directly to the Clinton/Gore presidential campaign during the 1995-1996 election cycle. The industry provided another US$2 million in "soft money" to the Democratic Party (CRP 1999). With the Vice President having declared his candidacy for the presidency in the year 2000, the loss of a potential US$2.1 million would have been a serious setback for his campaign, especially in light of Republican presidential candidate Governor George W. Bush's record-setting fundraising early in the campaign cycle. The Vice President, however, was not the only politician who had a financial interest in seeing the patent conflict resolved in favor of US interests.

In a letter dated February 2, 1999, forty-seven members of Congress urged USTR Charlene Barshefsky to "pursue all appropriate actions, including if necessary with the WTO." Campaign contributions data showed that thirty-four of the forty-seven members of Congress who signed the letter received financial support from the pharmaceutical and health industry that totaled US$298,742 (CRP 1999). The average contribution from the industry for the thirty-four members was US$8,786. In states and congressional districts that employ large numbers of constituents, the political persuasion carried by the industry was even stronger. The American electoral system makes financial support critical if incumbent politicians want reelection. It also provides a basis for those who seek policy changes, as Gore encountered while campaigning.

AIDS activists in the US brought the South African patent dispute directly to the campaign trail. They vowed to disrupt Gore's campaign until the US dropped its complaint against South Africa. The protestors were politically embarrassing for Gore, with hundreds of protestors turning out at campaign rallies for the Vice President (Richwine 1999; Ayres 1999). The protests had an impact on Gore and his stance on the issue. Because of the Vice President's view on the issue and the worsening of the AIDS crisis in South Africa, the Congressional Black Caucus asked the Vice President to update them on the situation in South Africa and to clarify his position on the patent issue. In a letter dated June 25 1999, Gore told the Chair of the Caucus, Representative James Clyburn, that "...I support South Africa's effort to provide AIDS drugs at reduced prices through compulsory licensing and parallel importing, so long as they are carried out in a way that is consistent with international agreements" (Gore 1999). Gore's view placed him directly in conflict with the pharmaceutical industry, which staunchly opposed parallel imports and compulsory licensing. In an effort to curb campaign protests, the Vice President released the letter publicly.

The message conveyed in the letter was one of understanding, which differed significantly from the US State Department's description of the administration's position. In a report to the House Committee on International Relations, Assistant Secretary for Legislative Affairs Barbara Larkin proclaimed that the US was involved "...in a full court press with South African officials" over the patent issue, making reference to the leading role that the Vice President had played in direct negotiations with Mbeki (United States State Department 1999). Little progress had been made in resolving the dispute, despite public commitment from Gore and Mbeki in seeking a mutually acceptable solution to the patent dispute.

By 2000, public pressure over the HIV/AIDS issue in Africa mounted in industrialized countries. Before the USTR could fully investigate the South African government's new pharmaceuticals law, President Clinton signed Executive Order 13155 (May 10, 2000), which forbid the USTR and other US government agencies from pursuing IPR violation cases against any sub-Saharan African country provided that the country was still in compliance with the TRIPS agreement. What this meant in practical terms was that sub-Saharan African countries could relax any patent restrictions that prevented them from utilizing generic substitutes and other mechanisms for lowering pharmaceutical prices. Clinton's executive order was followed by dramatic changes in the policies of the pharmaceutical industry.

In March 2001, the lawsuit filed by the industry went to court; however, the case turned immediately into a public relations disaster for the thirty-nine companies that had filed the suit. In a quick turnaround, the companies began a radical price-cutting program on their HIV/AIDS drugs for African countries. Before the court case could proceed, the pharmaceutical industry reached a tentative agreement with the South African government that would allow the new patent law to stand, but the government would only buy or make generic drugs in compliance with TRIPS. The PhRMA unconditionally withdrew its lawsuit and agreed to pay all costs associated with the case.

Conclusion

South Africa joined a list of countries that have drawn attention to the problem of patents for pharmaceuticals. Other countries such as Brazil, Argentina, and India have advocated a lessening of restrictions on the adoption of pharmaceuticals from abroad. The choice that South Africa and the developing world face is one of competing values: protecting those who create objects from being exploited by profiteers on the one hand, and alleviating personal suffering of people *when the capability to do so exists* on the other. The scenario is tantamount to a choice that the state has to make between protecting property rights and protecting subsistence rights. The government of South Africa was faced with a growing health crisis that threatened a large segment of its population. In short, the situation presented in the IPR dispute was a clash of northern economic interest versus southern social and economic needs, which was evident in the way the US addressed the issue with South Africa.

The USTR presented the PhRMA case as an issue of IPR protection. Nowhere in the complaint made by the USTR in the "Special 301" list did the USTR mention the underlying issues in South Africa's healthcare system. The USTR made no mention of the AIDS crisis, the legacy of apartheid, or the other associated problems. For the USTR, the issue was purely financial. The South African government, of course, had a much different perspective on the issue, emphasizing the AIDS epidemic as a social and human crisis with long-term consequences.

South Africa encountered the same problems other countries had experienced when the social and economic realities of developing countries collide head on with the economic interests of developed countries. The critical issue of pharmaceutical patents provided a glaring example of this problem. South Africa's future was challenged by two forces: the legacy of apartheid and the current AIDS crisis. The government moved in the direction that other countries did by compromising the guarantee of patents on critical pharmaceuticals. While there was no single answer to South Africa's AIDS crisis, less expensive solutions were and still are needed until a permanent solution to the HIV/AIDS epidemic is found.

Conclusion

The fundamental premise underlying this research has been that states behave differently in the international system given their development status. Developed and developing countries, because of their individual economic and political objectives, each pursue different policies toward their goals. Political factors temper and neutralize policies designed to achieve their respective goals. The research here clearly reflects this framework in the case of IPR protection and the ensuing conflict between developed and developing countries on the issue. Two questions formed the basis for this research: why do nations adopt strong intellectual property protection and what are the effects of adopting such policies?

One of the driving concepts in answering this question has been the emphasis on a state's level of development, which has a significant impact on the strength of IPR protection that a state is willing to extend. For a developed country with established high technology industries, a strong IPR regime is important in being able to sustain its position in highly competitive global markets. The most important factor in determining the level of IPR protection for developed states is their domestic technology levels. A strong positive relationship between technology levels and IPR protection emerged from the empirical analysis presented in chapter three. This finding lends credence to the notion that domestic pressure provides the incentive to maintain strong IPR protection at home while pursuing this type of IPR protection abroad. The developed countries, led by the US, have increasingly pushed for stronger IPR protection in the emerging markets of the developing world. The decision to pursue this objective was based on the need to limit economic competition and to maintain market shares for TNCs in these markets. Though the developed states have touted IPR protection as a benefit to all countries, the research presented here casts doubt on this orthodoxy.

The claims that strong IPR protection promotes economic growth have been examined empirically in this research. The results presented here differ from the first study by Gould and Gruben, who find a positive relationship between the two. Using the new measure of IPR protection developed in chapter two, scant evidence exists to support Gould and Gruben's findings that stronger IPR protection promotes economic growth. In fact, for less developed countries, the overall effect of IPR protection on economic growth may be negative. What this implies is that developing countries do not have the incentive to spend vital resources on the implementation of a full IPR system. Pressure must emerge, domestically or internationally, that could push states to adopt such policies, a conclusion supported by the empirical analysis of IPR protection.

Developing countries differed from developed countries regarding the protection of IPR in that developing countries have no domestic incentive to protect IPR, given their low levels of technological development. Greater exposure to the global economy establishes the foundation for developing countries to adopt greater IPR protection. Developing countries that trade more and accept large levels of foreign investment are more likely to endure greater international pressure to reform and enhance their IPR protection. Those countries that do have this exposure tend to be the moderately developed countries (as defined in the introduction) such as China, India, Argentina, Brazil, and Mexico. Least developed countries, such as El Salvador, Nigeria, Gabon, Nicaragua and Paraguay, which trade less and attract less foreign investment, will not be exposed to global pressures to adjust their IPR protection. The case studies of China and South Africa lend credible support to these findings.

The US case study documented a developed country's experience with IPR. Changes that promoted increased industrial competition in the global economy had an impact on three industries in the US: the pharmaceutical, software and entertainment industries. The government's response was to pressure other states to adopt stronger IPR protection for foreign producers. In doing so, the US government adopted a two-track approach to solving the issue: restricting imports that violated US IPR laws while pressuring other countries with trade sanctions into passing stronger IPR protection for US exports. But the US efforts internationally extended beyond domestic legislation to international fora, notably the GATT. Developing countries fiercely opposed what they perceived to be a US effort to impose its domestic legislation globally and to limit industrial competition. Despite the opposition, the United States persuaded the GATT general membership that the issue needed attention to maintain a healthy global trade system.

The case studies of China and South Africa illustrate similar scenarios through different circumstances. Both countries came under international pressure to adopt stronger IPR protection measures. For China, lax IPR protection was a means to support its economic growth, but for South Africa it was a means to support its battle against an epidemic. US interest groups, supported by the government, moved swiftly to reverse policies in each country when IPR violations began to affect them. In the case of China, the diplomatic wrangling sent Sino-American trade relations spiraling into the worst crisis since the US recognized China in the 1970s. For South Africa, the attention that US TNCs and the government lent to the IPR issue backfired in the "court of public opinion." Public pressure forced TNCs and the US government to backpedal from their demand that South Africa tighten its patent protection, which would restrict access to life-saving HIV/AIDS retroviral medication.

Implications

In part, politics and the study of politics are concerned about resource allocations: who gets what and why? For less developed countries, the IPR issue is not only financial but it is also clearly a political issue. Should they take vital resources that could be expended on human needs and other areas and spend them on the promotion of a full IPR system? Theoretically, I argued in chapter one that to place industrial profits above human needs presents ethical issues that warrant closer scrutiny of the IPR issue, particularly for states at the lower end of the development spectrum. Moreover, those ethical issues warrant a critical examination of policies using sanctions and diplomatic pressure to coerce developing countries to act contrarily to their own interests and needs. When trade is combined with the IPR issue, developing states can be coerced into domestic IPR policy that mitigates against their needs; this is the development dilemma that developing states face.

The overall benefits for a developing country promoting a strong IPR regime are in doubt as the empirical evidence presented here shows that the effects are marginal or even negative. Hence, until they are able to sustain industrial development, these countries may be better served by adopting weaker protection for IPR. Historical evidence, even from the US experience, supports such a prescription. By doing developing countries can acquire technology and products contribute to building a sustainable industrial sector produces both tangible and intangible products. In cases of conflict between developed and developing countries, developing countries must balance international pressure for IPR protection against the gains to domestic industry from pirating technology. How developing states move out of the development dilemma varies. There will be some point where the benefits of a weak IPR regime will not outweigh the costs associated with losses inflicted by trade sanctions or domestic costs in terms of lost incentives to produce IPR-dependent products. This point, however, is unique to each country and is subject to constant review by policymakers based on that country's development.

Developed countries are faced with two issues in deciding their IPR policy. First are the domestic concerns. Industrial development is high, which means that competition will be based more on what may be referred to as "cutting-edge" technology. Entrepreneurs will both demand and need the protection of that technology from domestic duplication, but the issue does not stop there. Domestic markets often are saturated with new products and eventually products are exported to maintain expanding profits and to generate additional research revenues. Businesses, however, face a different legal climate in foreign countries. This is where the second concern appears. As a matter of policy, governments of developed countries try to protect industry IPR in foreign markets. This policy is important for sustained growth and production and for the control of sensitive technologies. Hence, governments are rational in seeking IPR protection for their industries in export markets.

The different approaches to IPR protection will, eventually, disappear. The TRIPS agreement administered under the World Trade

Organization mandates minimum IPR protection for all signatory countries. Over time, developing countries will need to adopt minimum IPR protection to comply with their TRIPS obligations. Thus, the only flexibility all states will have in adjusting their policies will be in the enforcement of these new laws. Some countries may just disregard the laws. Other countries may not be able to sustain the institutions needed to enforce the laws, such as courts for trials, arbitration panels or customs inspection. The result could be a loss of trade privileges that would perpetuate economic problems faced by many countries.

While the different policies toward IPR are rational, given the goals and development levels of countries in the international order, they do not begin to address the ethical and moral issues when the goals of developed and developing countries collide. At a general level, what I have argued is that rational policies have moral implications that do not stand alone in a political vacuum. They have consequences. In the case of IPR protection, the strict enforcement of IPR laws has consequences that extend beyond the market and touch the daily lives of people. Of particular concern is the implication that strong IPR protection has the potential to put profits above issues of human subsistence. As such, modifications to the policies that each country should adopt are warranted. The question that needs to be addressed in such modifications is: what is an appropriate balance between the right to profit and the right to human subsistence. What complicates this issue most is the disparity among the countries of the world in terms of their economic capacity to pay for services and goods needed to sustain their populations.

In the long term, it is in the interest of the developed countries to aid the developing countries to open and to maintain new markets. By not pressuring the governments of developing countries into strict IPR protection policies, the governments of developed countries will be assisting in constructing vibrant consumer markets. The result can only benefit all those concerned in the IPR issue. Ultimately, the development of consumer markets will bring with it the domestic demand for IPR protection. By this point, the governments of developing countries may be better positioned economically and politically to sustain such a policy. Hence, short-term patience and assistance may result in long-term gains for everyone.

Measurement Appendix

Measuring Intellectual Property Laws

Based on the US Chamber of commerce minimal criteria guidelines for intellectual property right laws, I created code sheets for trademark, patent and copyright laws. Three separate coders (myself and two assistants) coded these laws for the three time periods, 1988, 1991, and 1994. I then calculated inter-coder agreement scores (calculated as the number of items coders disagreed upon as a percentage of total possible items on the code sheets), These scores were all .90 or higher, indicating that the errors among the coders were 10% or less for each set of coding. The items on the code sheet were mostly dichotomous (either the law accommodated the provision or it did not); those that were not dichotomous were converted to dichotomous items in order to simplify the scaling process.

All the individual items for each type of law were then brought together and a measure of association, the gamma coefficient, was calculated for each pair of items. I calculated the gamma coefficients (Yule's-Q with dichotomous data) for a 2 x 2contingency table using the formula

$$Q = \frac{ad - bc}{ad + bc}$$

where the contingency table is as follows:

a	b
c	d

A search for scales or clusters was then performed. Clusters were defined as those paired items with a gamma coefficient at .80 or higher. Because all the items from the three types of laws combined did not possess sufficient numbers of coefficients above .80, I was able to conclude that the three types of laws are not highly associated. The clustering that did occur was within the three types of laws. Gamma coefficients were then analyzed within the three types of laws and it was determined that these clusters would scale sufficiently with coefficients above .80 in most cases. Items that did not cluster together within the three types of laws were discarded in accordance with standard procedures (MacRae 1970).

The remaining items within each law were then summated across the rows and columns in accordance with Guttman scaling procedures. The columns were then sorted from highest to lowest by summated totals.

Guttman Scaling Methodology

Guttman scaling (scalogram analysis or cumulative scaling) is a deterministic model of scaling designed to order both items and subjects with some respect to some underlying cumulative dimension. A perfect Guttman scale can be seen in this example taken from McIver and Carmines (1981)

	Items						
Subjects	1	2	3	4	5	6	**Scale Score**
A	1	1	1	1	1	1	6
B	1	1	1	1	1	0	5
C	1	1	1	1	0	0	4
D	1	1	1	0	0	0	3
E	1	1	0	0	0	0	2
F	1	0	0	0	0	0	1
G	0	0	0	0	0	0	0

From the scale, we should be able to predict accurately the subject's response to each of the dichotomous items that make up the scale. Scalogram analysis, however, assumes that this pattern of responses will be violated in some form. The focus at this point is on how much deviation is acceptable to the researcher and how these deviations affect the scalability of the items. The next task was to calculate the deviations and determine the acceptable levels of deviations in the three scales.

Guttman Scale Error Counting Procedures

With the intellectual property right law items arranged in this pattern, I began the search for errors in the pattern. Errors in this sense are defined as deviations from the observed response pattern with the ideal response pattern in the cumulative model (McIver and Carmines 1981, 42). An illustration of this process is below.

	Items						
Subjects	1	2	3	4	5	6	**Scale Score**
A	1	1	1	1	1	1	6
B	1	1	1	1	1	0	5
C	1	1	0	1	0	1	4
D	1	1	1	0	0	0	3
E	1	1	0	0	0	0	2
F	1	0	0	0	0	0	1
G	0	0	0	0	0	0	0

For subject C, with a scale score of 4, we would expect that there would be positive responses to the first four items. However, the third item has a negative response, while the sixth item has a positive response. Under the Goodenough-Edwards technique of error counting (deviations from perfect reproducibility) , two errors for the item are assigned-- one for the negative response in item three and one for the positive response in item six.

This procedure was performed for all three laws. A coefficient of reproducibility (CR) was used to assess the scalability of the items for the three laws. The CR is a measure of the errors in the scales as a percentage of total responses (CR= 1-(# errors)/(total responses). Guttman suggests that scales should be constructed with a CR at .90 or higher, indicating an acceptable error rate of 10% or less. All the CR scores for the three laws were above .90. Scale scores were then assigned by summing across all items for each respondent. Because it is recognized that the Goodenough-Edwards technique of error counting is a strict criteria for error counting, the CR based on this error counting technique is considered to be conservative (McIver and Carmines, 1991, 48). Next, a coefficient of scalability (CS) was calculated in order to account for the possibility that the item marginals may be skewed regardless of the items relationships. The CS is calculated as (1 - (scale errors)/(marginal errors)). Marginal errors are defined as the sum of all nonmodal frequencies. Though not theoretically justified in any manner, a CS of .60 or higher is used as a rule of thumb as an indication of scalability. All CS scores were .60 or above for all laws in all years. All scores and calculations appear on the next page.

Reliability and Stability Coefficients

These measures represent reliability and stability for panel designs. Given that I am looking at the same countries over the same period of time, these statistics were appropriate for determining the reliability and stability of the IPR measures.

Heise (1971) examines these coefficients in detail in his article. In short the measures are calculated as follows:

1. The Pearson correlations among all three waves are taken for each variable
2. For the reliability coefficient, the following formula is applied:

$$r_{xx} = \frac{r_{88-91} r_{91-94}}{r_{88-94}}$$

where each correlation is between the years specified by the subscripts. The proofs for this formula are presented in Heise's (1971) work.

3. For the stability coefficient, the following formulae are applied:

$$s_{88-91} = r_{88-94}/r_{91-94}$$
$$s_{91-94} = r_{88-94}/r_{88-91}$$

$$s_{88\text{-}94} = (r_{88\text{-}94})^2/(r_{88\text{-}91})(r_{91\text{-}94})$$

As such, these represent stability of the measures over the specified periods associated with the coefficients. Again, Heise (1971) provides proof of these.

Notes

Chapter One

* A version of this chapter appeared first in the journal *Human Rights Quarterly as* Ostergard, Robert L. 1999. "Intellectual Property Rights: A Universal Human Right?" *Human Rights Quarterly* Vol. 21 No. 1: 156-178. I am grateful to the editors for granting permission to reprint it here.

1. The interpretation of Locke's labor theory and the two provisos has been the subject of much literature in political theory. I do not wish to enter the debate on the interpretation of these ideas only in that I have chosen interpretations that are common in the IPR literature.
2. Nozick does not address the nature of intellectual property as private property; however it is clear in his work that an individual who possesses the talents to produce an intellectual object is entitled to possession.
3. While this on the surface seems to be a moot point in that the profit motive should entice firms to make their products available to all people, some examples show that this is not necessarily the case. For instance, the elderly and the critically ill often find themselves unable to afford medicines needed to sustain their lives.
4. This scenario is not at all fantasy. Consider the case of Dr. Samuel Pallin, who has applied for a patent and subsequently demanded royalties (though marginal) for an opthamalogical surgical procedure (New York Times, June 8, 1995, D1).

5. I am ignoring, of course, the neo-Marxist arguments that directly attack developed countries and multinational corporations for their role in creating the impoverished conditions in much of the developing world (Galtung 1973; Dos Santo 1970; Frank 1966; Packenham 1992).

Chapter Two

* Parts of this chapter originally appeared in the *Journal of International Business Studies* as Ostergard, Robert L. 2000. "The Measurement of Intellectual Property Rights Protection." *Journal of International Business Studies* Vol. 31 No. 2: 349-360. I am grateful to the editors for granting permission to reprint it.

1. This date includes the 10-year exception for implementation of the agreement's provisions by developing countries established in Article 65 of the agreement. The full text of the TRIPS agreement can be found at the World Trade Organization web site at http://www.wto.org/english/docs_e/legal_e/final_e.htm#TRIPs.
2. The technical description of the methodologies employed in this section can be found in the Measurement Appendix to the book.
3. While not perfect, content analysis provides set criteria for coding elements, making the coding less subjective. Of course, it does not eliminate subjectivity in deciding what to code. For a classic statement on content analysis, see Krippendorf 1980
4. The countries were determined by the countries listed in the initial editions of the State Department's *Country Reports on Economic and Trade Practices*. The other coders were research assistants independent of the author.
5. The proof of this follows from logarithmic transformations. In using the IPR protection variables in a linear regression, the equation is $Y = \propto + \beta_1(\text{laws} \cdot \text{enforcement})$. By logarithmic transformation, the equation becomes

$$\text{Log}_e Y = \propto + \beta_1 \text{Log}_e(\text{Laws}) + \beta_2 \text{Log}_e(\text{Enforcement})$$

and when this equation is restated with respect to Y, the retransformed version of the log equation is

$$Y = e^{\alpha} (\{Laws^{\beta 1}\}\{Enforcement^{\beta 2}\})$$

The beta coefficients become the weights of each component of the IPR protection score.

6. Gould and Gruben use a log function in their analysis for two reasons. First, the function has a base in standard economic production function literature. Second, the log function will minimize the mean squared error (Gould and Gruben 330).

Chapter Four

1. The debate over convergence theory emerged around 1986 from the work of Abramovitz. (See Abramovitz, M. 1986. "Catching Up, Forging Ahead and Falling Behind." The Journal of Economic History XLVI (2): 385-406). Abramovitz presented evidence for convergence between 1870-1979. While convergence theory postulates that all nations would eventually converge, with the least developed countries having the highest growth rates and the developed countries the lowest, the evidence of such convergence is not strong. The evidence for convergence has occurred mainly among the richest of the middle income countries (See Baumol, W. 1986. "Productivity Growth, Convergence, and Welfare." American Economic Review December (76): 1072-85). Others have claimed that Baumol's findings are suspect, contaminated by selection bias (See DeLong, J. B., 1996. "Productivity: Growth and Convergence." in International Political Economy: State-Market Relations in the Changing Global Order, ed. C. R. Goddard, J. T. Passe-Smith and J. G. Conklin Boulder, Lynne Rienner). When the bias is removed, so is the evidence for convergence (See Passe-Smith, J. T. 1996. "Convergence and Divergence in the Post World-War II Era." in International Political Economy: State-Market Relations in the Changing Global Order. ed. C. R. Goddard, J. T. Passe-Smith and J. G. Conklin. Boulder, Lynne Rienner).
2. "Unjustifiable" practices are restrictions which are illegal under international law or inconsistent with international obligations. "Unreasonable" restrictions are those which are not necessarily illegal but which nullify or impair benefits accruing to the United States under trade agreements or which otherwise discriminate

against or burden US companies (See United States Code. 1974. Congressional and Administrative News. 93rd Congress, Second Session, Trade Act of 1974. St. Paul: West Publishing. 4: 7186+).

3. Even during this period, patents were not much of a concern until the late 1940s and early 1950s. Early in American history, patents were not granted to pharmaceuticals on ethical grounds and doctors who did manage to get pharmaceutical items patented were looked upon with suspicion (see Noonan, W. D. 1990. "Patenting Medical Technology." Journal of Legal Medicine 11: 263-319).
4. Outsourcing has become a major issue in labor relations in the United States. This practice involves contracting production jobs out to third party producers as lower costs, allowing the manufacturer to cut labor costs. Recent labor strikes in the auto industry have been conducted to fight outsourcing of production jobs to cheaper labor companies.
5. This situation is exactly what did happen. Developing countries ultimately bargained to get foreign market access for their manufactured products in exchange for stronger IPR protection in their domestic markets during the Uruguay Round of the GATT.
6. "Statement of Brazil to the Negotiating Group on Trade-Related Aspects of Intellectual Property Rights, including Trade in Counterfeit Goods" to the GATT working group on Trade Related Intellectual Property Rights, 25 March 1987 cited in Gadbaw and Gwynn, 1988, p. 41.
7. General Accounting Office 1987. The US Trade Deficit: Causes and Policy Options for Solutions (Report to Congressional Requesters, NO GAO/NSIAD-87-135.)
8. Administration Memo of May 7, 1987. "Objectionable Provisions in S. 490 as approved by the Senate Finance Committee, May 7, 1987." in Inside US Trade. "Section 301 Provisions Head White House Objections to Senate Trade Bill," May 22, 1987.
9. The Super 301 provision requires a dollar for dollar retaliation against any country using unfair trade practices. The USTR identifies countries that have "priority practices," which include trade barriers that pose the greatest hindrance US exports.
10. The Section 301 Committee is composed of the USTR, representatives from cabinet departments (Labor, State, Treasury, Defense, Interior, Commerce, Justice, Agriculture and the Office of Management and Budget), the National Security Council and the Council of Economic Advisors (Phillips 1989).

11. Those conditions included: (1) GATT decisions that trade agreements had not been violated; (2) the country takes measures to grant trade agreement rights; (3) the country agrees to eliminate the practice; (4) the country provides the US with compensatory benefits (Phillips 1989; Anonymous Personal Interview March 27, 1997).
12. Priority countries are defined by one of three conditions: (1) countries that have the most egregious acts, policies or practices that deny adequate and effective protection of intellectual property rights; (2) countries whose acts, policies or practices deny adequate and effective protection of intellectual property rights have the greatest adverse impact in their own markets, or in other international markets, for the affected United States items; and (3) countries that have not entered into good faith negotiations, or are not making significant progress in bilateral or multilateral negotiations, to provide adequate and effective protection of intellectual property (see Bello, J. H. and A. F. Holmer, (1990). "The Heart of the 1988 Trade Act: A Legislative History of the Amendments to Section 301." in Aggressive Unilateralism: America's 301 Trade Policy and the World Trading System,. ed. J. Bhagwati and H. T. Patrick Ann Arbor, University of Michigan Press.

    Priority watch list countries are those that the USTR has identified as having IPR inadequacies, but are making efforts unilaterally or in conjunction with international organizations or the US to improve the situation. The US may also be pursuing dispute resolution measures against these countries with international organizations such as the World Trade Organization.

    Watch countries are those that are implementing commitments with regard to IPR protection or have been initially cited with new developments that effect their IPR protection. In this sense, the list acts as a way for the US to monitor other countries' progress in complying with intellectual property rights obligations

13. Special 301 provided three conditions that allowed the president to refrain from imposing penalties. First, if a GATT complaint had been filed, the GATT findings would override the need for retaliation. So, if a GATT decision found that US property rights had not been violated, the president could legitimately back away

retaliation. Second, if the USTR finds that significant progress was being made, the president could delay retaliatory penalties against the country (Berliner 1990: 736). Likewise, if the country agreed to stop the practice, the president could rescind retaliatory action. The latter two provisions provided significant retaliatory discretion to both the USTR and the president.

Chapter Five

1. This was more than two thousand years before European "development" of the IP concept which was later used to bolster imperial power.

Chapter Six

* This chapter originally appeared in the *Journal of World Intellectual Property* as Ostergard, Robert L. 1999. "The Political Economy of the South African-US Patent Conflict" *Journal of World Intellectual Property* Vol. 2. No. 4.: 875-888. I am grateful to the editors for their permission to reprint it.

1. It is important to note the difference between HIV prevalence and HIV incidence. Studies of HIV prevalence data are for one specified period of time; HIV incidence data covers an extended period of time. Hence, HIV incidence data are more stable and reliable over time and across groups. Because of the inherent data collection problems and lack of systematic record keeping in Africa, most often data reported are prevalence data, making estimates of the extent of infection difficult to asses.

Data References

The following sources were used in creating the dataset used in chapters two and three.

Banks, Arthur S. 1996. *Cross-National Time Series Data Archive.* Binghamton: Arthur S. Banks.

Hemnes, Thomas M. S., Mara G. DiMambro, and Marcia L. Moore. 1993. *Intellectual Property World Desk Reference: A Guide to Practice by Country, State and Province.* Boston: Kluwer Law and Taxation Publishers.

Jabobs, Alan J. and Elizabeth Hanellin, eds. 1997. *Patents Throughout the World. 4th Ed.* New York: Clark Boardman Callaghan.

National Association of Credit Management. 1975. *Digest of Commercial Laws of the World: Patent and Trademarks Vols. I and II.* ed. George Kohlik. New York: Oceana Publications.

Politi, Jeanine M (ed). 1996. *Trademarks Throughout the World.* New York: Clark Boardman Callaghan.

Protecting Intellectual Property in Asia-Pacific. 1989. Melbourne: Longman Cheshire Pty. Limited.

United Nations Educational, Scientific and Cultural Organization. 1956. *Copyright Laws and Treaties of the World.* United Nations: Paris.

United States State Department. 1989-1995 (annual reports) *Country Reports on Economic and Trade Practices*. Superintendent of Documents: Washington DC.

The World Bank. 1997. *World Development Indicators* [cd-rom]. Washington DC: The World Bank

The World Bank. 1988-1997. *World Development Report*. Washington DC: World Bank.

World Intellectual Property Rights Organization. 1990. *Industrial Property Laws and Treaties* WIPO: Geneva.

References

Abbott, Frederick M. 1989. "Protecting First World Assets in the Third World: Intellectual Property Negotiations in the GATT Multilateral Framework." *Vanderbilt Journal of Transnational Law* 22:689-745.

Abramovitz, M. 1986. "Catching Up, Forging Ahead and Falling Behind." *The Journal of Economic History* 46:385-406.

Ackiron, Evan. 1991. "Patents for Critical Pharmaceuticals." *American Journal of Law and Medicine* 17, no. 145.

Alford, William P. 1995. *To Steal a Book is an Elegant Offense: Intellectual Property Law in Chinese Civilization.* Stanford: Stanford University Press.

Anonymous. 1997. Department of State, Personal Interview. March 27.

Arthur, John. 1996. "Rights and the Duty to Bring Aid." In *World Hunger and Morality*, ed. William Aiken and Hugh LaFollette. Upper Saddle River NJ: Prentice Hall.

Ayres, B. Drummond. 1999. "Gore Is Followed By AIDS Protesters." *New York Times*, July 2: A12.

Baleta, Adele. 1999. "South African Government Faces Furious Zidovudine Debate (News)." *The Lancet* 353(9156): 908.

Band, J., and M. Katoh. 1995. *Interfaces on Trial: Intellectual Property and Interoperability in the Global Software Industry.* Boulder: Westview Press.

Baumol, W. 1986. "Productivity Growth, Convergence, and Welfare." *American Economic Review* 76:1072-85.

Bayard, T. O., and K. A. Elliott. 1994. *Reciprocity and Retaliation in US Trade Policy*. Washington: Institute for International Economics.

Bello, J. H., and A. F. Holmer. 1990. "The Heart of the 1988 Trade Act: A Legislative History of the Amendments to Section 301." In *Aggressive Unilateralism: America's 301 Trade Policy and the World Trading System*, ed. J. Bhagwati and H. T. Patrick. Ann Arbor: University of Michigan Press.

Benatar, Solomon R. 1997. "An Old Health Care System Gives Place to New." *The Lancet*, May 24.

Benko, Robert P. 1987. *Protecting Intellectual Property: Issues and Controversies*. Washington: American Enterprise Institute for Public Policy Research.

Berliner, B. M. 1990. "Making Intellectual Property Pirates Walk the Plank: Using "Special 301" to Protect United States' Rights." *Loyola of Los Angeles International and Comparative Law Journal* 12:725-752.

Besen, Stanley M. and Leo J. Raskind. 1991. "An Introduction to the Law and Economics of Intellectual Property" *The Journal of Economic Perspectives*, Vol. 5. 1: 3-27.

Bhagwati, J. 1990. "Aggressive Unilateralism: An Overview." In *Aggressive Unilateralism: America's 301 Trade Policy and the World Trading System*, ed. J. Bhagwati and H. T. Patrick. Ann Arbor: University of Michigan Press.

Bugbee, Bruce W. 1967. *The Genesis of American Patent and Copyright Law*. Washington: Public Affairs Press.

Campbell, R. M. 1976. "The Foreign Trade Aspects of the Trade Act of 1974, Pt II." *Washington and Lee Law Review* 33:639-699.

Center for Responsive Politics. 1999. Political Action Committees. Accessed June 29. Available from http://www.opensecrets.org/pacs/index.htm.

Chi, Shaojie. 1996. "Border Enforcement of Intellectual Property Rights in China." *International Review of Industrial Property* 27:490-494.

Chien-Hale, Elizabeth. 1997. "Asserting US Intellectual Property Rights in China: Expansion of Extraterritorial Jurisdiction." *Journal of the Copyright Society of the USA* 44:198-230.

Cohen, I. 1995. *Science and the Founding Fathers*. New York: W W Norton & Co.

Comanor, William S. 1986. "The political economy of the Pharmaceutical Industry." *Journal of Economic Literature*, Vol. 24, No. 3: 1178-1217.

DeLong, J. B. 1996. "Productivity: Growth and Convergence." In *International Political Economy: State-Market Relations in the Changing Global Order,* ed. C. R. Goddard, J.T. Passe-Smith, and J. G. Conklin. Boulder: Lynne Riener.

Destler, I. M. 1992. *American Trade Politics*. Washington: Institute for International Economics.

Dhar, B. 1992. "The Decline of Free Trade and US Trade Policy Today." *Journal of World Trade* 26:133-154.

Dos Santos, Theotonio 1970. "The Structure of Dependence." *The American Economic Review*, May:231-236.

Ebanks, K. D. 1989. "Pirates of the Caribbean Revisited: An Examination of the Continuing Problem of Satellite Signal Piracy in the Caribbean and Latin America." *Law and Policy in International Business* 21:33-52.

Eliason, Scott R. 1993. *Maximum Likelihood Estimation: Logic and Practice* (Sage University Paper series on Quantitative Applications in the Social Sciences, no. 07-096). Newbury Park, CA: Sage.

Endeshaw, Assafa. 1996. "A Critical Assessment of the US-China Conflict on Intellectual Property." *Albany Law Journal of Science and Technology*. 6:295-337.

Engardio, P., and D. Roberts. 1996. "Microsoft's Long March." *Business Week*, June 24.

Fairbanks, John K., Edwin O. Reischauer, and Albert M. Craig. 1978. *East Asia: Tradition and Transformation*. Boston: Houghton Mifflin Co.

Foreign Broadcast Information Service (FBIS). 1996. "Foreign Trade and Investment: PRC: Roundup of IPR-Related Reports 9 Jun-5 Jul." FBIS-CHI-96-140, July 19.

Frame, J. Davidson. 1984. "Problems in the Use of Literature-based S&T Indicators in Developing Countries." In *Hiroko Morita-Lou (1984) Science and Technology Indicators for Development*. Boulder: Westview Press.

--1987. "National Commitment to Intellectual Property." *Journal of Law and Technology* 2:209-227.

Frank, Andre Gunder. 1966. "The Development of Underdevelopment." *Monthly Review*, September 17-31.

Frieden, Jeffry A. 1991. *Debt Development and Democracy: Modern Political Economy and Latin America, 1965-1985*. Princeton: Princeton University Press.

Frisbie, W. P., and C. J. Clarke. 1979. "Technology in evolutionary and ecological perspective: Theory and measurement at the societal level." *Social Forces* 63:750-766.

Fusco, Thomas S. 1997. Investigative Attorney United States International Trade Commission personal interview, United States International Trade Commission. Washington. March 25.

Gadbaw, R. Michael, and Rosemary E. Gwynn. 1988. "Intellectual Property Rights in the New GATT Round." In *Intellectual Property Rights: Global Consensus, Global Conflict?* ed. R. Michael Gadbaw and Timothy J. Richards. Boulder: Westview Press.

Galtung, Johan. 1971. "A Structural Theory of Imperialism." *Journal of Peace Research* 2:81-117.

Garson, David. 1976. *Handbook of Political Science Methods 2nd Ed.* Boston: Holbrooke Press.

Goldstein, Paul. 1994. *Copyright's Highway: The Law and Lore of Copyright from Gutenberg to the Celestial Jukebox*. New York: Hill and Wang.

Gore, Albert. 1999. "Correspondence to Representative James E. Clyburn."

Gould, David M., and William C. Gruben. 1996. "The Role of Intellectual Property Rights in Economic growth." *Journal of Development Economics* 48:323-350.

Green, L. D. 1989. "International Protection of Intellectual Property Under the 1988 Trade Bill." *Brigham Young University Law Review* 2:475-490.

Gurr, Ted R., and Keith Jaggers. 1995. "Tracking Democracy's Third Wave with the Polity III Data." *Journal of Peace Research* 32:469-482.

--1996. Polity III [computer file]: regime type and political authority, 1800-1994. Ann Arbor: Inter-University Consortium for Political and Social Research [distributor].

Gutterman, Alan S. 1993. "The North-South Debate Regarding the Protection of Intellectual Property Rights." *Wake Forest Law Review* 28:89-139.

Haggard, Stephan. 1990. *Pathways from the Periphery*. Ithaca: Cornell University Press.

Harrison, B., and B. Bluestone. 1988. *The Great U-Turn: Corporate Restructuring and the Polarizing of America*. New York: Basic Books

Heeks, R. 1996. *India's Software Industry: State Policy, Liberalisation and Industrial Development*. New Delhi: Sage Publications.

Heise, David R. 1971. "Separating Reliability and Stability in Test-Retest Correlation." In *Causal Models in the Social Sciences*, ed. H. M. Blalock, Jr. Chicago: Aldine Atherton.

Herzfeld, Shannon S. S. 1999. "Identification of Countries Under Section 182 (Special 301) of the Trade Act of 1974, as amended, in response to USTR's Federal Register Notice." Pharmaceutical Research and Manufacturers of America (PhRMA).

Hettinger, Edwin C. 1989. "Justifying Intellectual Property." *Philosophy and Public Affairs* 18:31-52.

Hobson, J. A. 1948. *Imperialism, A Study*. London: G. Allen & Unwin Ltd.

Hughes, Justin. 1988. "The Philosophy of Intellectual Property." *The Georgetown Law Review*. 77:287-366.

Inside US Trade. 1986. "Brazil's President Rescinds Software Rules Meant to Curb Imports." October 3:7.

Inside US Trade. 1986. "US and Brazil Tackle Most Controversial Trade Issue Next Month." November 21:1, 14-16.

Inside US Trade. 1986. "US Probes Brazilian Intellectual Property Protection; Possible Import Curbs." November 21:14.

Inside US Trade. 1986. "USTR Draft on Intellectual Property Shows Failure of Bilateral Approach." January 24:1, 7-10.

Inside US Trade. 1987. "Congress Increases Pressure on Brazil to Open Market to US Computers." 19:5, May 8:1.

Inside US Trade. 1987. "Section 301 Provisions Head White House Objections to Senate Trade Bill." May 22, Special Report.

Inside US Trade. 1988. "Administration to Push for GATT Intellectual Property Rules in Next Two Years." November 25:7-8.

Inside US Trade. 1988. "Highly Influential Group Was to Meet with GATT Officials." Jan 29:17.

International Monetary Fund. 1998. "Direction of Trade Statistics." Washington: International Monetary Fund.

Jochelson, Karen. 1999. "Sexually Transmitted Diseases in Nineteenth and Twentieth Century South Africa." In *Histories of Sexually Transmitted Diseases and HIV/AIDS in Sub-Saharan Africa*, ed. Philip Setel, Milton James Lewis, and Maryinez Lyons. Westport CT: Greenwood Press.

Kale, Rajendra. 1995. "Restructuring South Africa's Health Care: Dilemmas for Planners (South Africa's Health, part 5)." *British Medical Journal 310* 6991:1397-1399.

Keohane, Robert. 1984. *After Hegemony*. Princeton: Princeton University Press.

Kindleberger, C. P. 1981. "Dominance and Leadership in the International Economy: Exploitation, Public Goods, and Free Rides." *International Studies Quarterly* 25:242-255.

King, Gary. 1989. *Unifying Political Methodology: The Likelihood Theory of Statistical Inference*. Cambridge, England and New York: Cambridge University Press.

Kleinbaum, David G. 1994. *Logistic Regression: A Self-Learning Text.* Springer Verlag.

Kleinschmidt, I. "South African Tuberculosis Mortality Data - Showing the First Signs of the AIDS Epidemic?." *South African Medical Journal* 89(3): 269-273.

Kmenta, Jan. 1986. *Elements of Econometrics*. New York: MacMillan.

Krasner, Stephen D. 1983. *International Regime*. Ithaca: Cornell University Press.

Kuznets, Simon. 1972. "Innovations and Adjustments in Economic Growth." *Swedish Journal of Economics* 4:431-451.

Kymlicka, Will. 1990. *Contemporary Political Philosophy: An Introduction.* Oxford: Clarendon Press.

Lall, Sanjaya. 1976. "The Patent System and the Transfer of Technology to Less-Developed Countries." *Journal of World Trade Law* 10:1-16.

Laqueur, Walter, and Barry Rubin. 1989. *The Human Rights Reader*. New York: Meridian.

Lewis-Beck, Michael S. 1980. *Applied Regression: An Introduction*. (Sage University Paper series on Quantitative Applications in the Social Sciences, no. 07-022). Newbury Park, CA: Sage

Liao, Tim Futing. 1994. *Interpreting Probability Models: Logit, Probit, and Other Generalized Linear Models.* (Sage University Paper series on Quantitative Applications in the Social Sciences, no. 07-101). Newbury Park, CA: Sage

Locke, John. 1988. *Two Treatises of Government*, ed. Peter Laslett. Cambridge: Cambridge University Press.

MacRae, Duncan Jr. 1970. *Issues and Parties in Legislative Voting: Methods and Statistical Analysis*. New York: Harper and Row.

Malecki, Edward J. 1991. *Technology and Economic Development: The Dynamics of Local, Regional, and National Change*. New York: Longman Scientific and Technical.

Mansfield, Edwin. 1990. "Intellectual Property, Technology, and Economic Growth." In *Intellectual Property Rights in Science, Technology, and Economic Performance*, ed. Francis W. Rushing and Carole Ganz Brown. Boulder: Westview Press.

Marshall, P. G. 1993. "Software Piracy: Can the Government Help Stop the Drain on Profits?" *CQ Researcher* 19(3): 434-455.

May, D. K. 1991. "Pharmaceutical Crisis in India: Transcending Profits with Human Rights." *Wisconsin International Law Journal* 10:40-77.

McKiver, John P., and Edward G. Carmines. 1981. *Unidimensional Scaling*. Beverly Hills: Sage Publications.

Morris, Morris. 1979. *Measuring the Condition of the World's Poor: The Physical Quality of Life Index*. New York: Pergamon Press.

Mutti, J. 1993. "Intellectual Property Protection in the United States under Section 337." *The World Economy* 16:339-357.

National Assembly of South Africa. 1997. Medicines and Related Substances Control Amendment Act, No. 90.

Nelson, R. R., 1990. "What Has Happened to US Technological Leadership?" In *Technological Competition and Interdependence: The Search for Policy in the United States, West Germany and Japan*, ed. G. Heiduk and K. Yamamura. Spokane: University of Washington Press.

Nelson, R. R., and G. Wright. 1992. "The Rise and Fall of American Technological Leadership." *Journal of Economic Literature* 30:1931-1964.

Nevin, Tom. 1998. "Will AIDS Kill Africa's Economy?" *African Business* 230:16-19.

Newman, A. S. 1989. "The Amendments to Section 337: Increased Protection for Intellectual Property Rights." *Law and Policy in International Business* 20:571-588.

Nogues, J. 1990. "Patents and Pharmaceutical Drugs: Understanding the Pressures on Developing Countries." *Journal of World Trade* 24:81-104.

Noonan, W. D. 1990. "Patenting Medical Technology." *Journal of Legal Medicine* 11:263-319.

Nozick, Robert. 1974. *Anarchy, State, and Utopia*. New York: Basic Books.

Okun, Arthur K. 1980. "Rights and Dollars." In *Property Profits and Economic Justice*, ed. Virginia Held. Belmont: Wadsworth.

Ostergard, Robert. 1999. "Intellectual Property Rights: A Universal Human Right?" *Human Rights Quarterly* 21(1): 156-178.

Packenham, Robert. 1992. *The Dependency Movement: Scholarship and Politics in Development Studies*. Cambridge: Harvard University Press.

Packard, Randall M. 1989. *White Plague, Black Labor: Tuberculosis and the Political Economy of Health and Disease in South Africa - Comparative Studies of Health Systems and Medical Care*. Berkeley: University of California Press.

Palmer, Tom G. 1993. *Intellectual Property Rights: Moral Philosophy and Ideal Objects*. Masters Thesis. The Catholic University of America.

Passe-Smith, J. T., 1996. "Convergence and Divergence in the Post World-War II Era." In *International Political Economy: State-Market Relations in the Changing Global Order*, ed. C. R. Goddard, J. T. Passe-Smith and J. G. Conklin. Boulder: Lynne Riener.

Pastor, R. A. 1980. *Congress and the Politics of US Foreign Economic Policy.* Berkeley: University of California Press.

Patel, Surendra, ed. 1983. *Pharmaceuticals and Health in the Third World.* Oxford: Pergamon Press.

Penrose, Edith Tilton. 1951. *The Economics of the International Patent System.* Baltimore: The Johns Hopkins University Press.

Phillips, S. 1989. "The New Section 301 of the Omnibus Trade and Competitiveness Act of 1988: Trade Wars or Open Markets?" *Vanderbilt Journal of Transnational Law* 22:491-579.

Pirt, N. E. 1987. "Regulation of the Export of Pharmaceuticals to Developing Countries." *Duquesne Law Review*, Winter.

Prozesky, O. W. 1993. "AIDS and Its Consequences for Southern Africa." In *Health in Africa*, ed. G. S. Fehrsen. Potchefstroom, South Africa: Potchefstroom University for Christian Higher Education.

Purvis, A. 1996. "The Goodwill Pill Mess." *Time*, April 29.

Raghavan, Chakravarthi. 1990. *Recolonization: GATT, the Uruguay Round & the Third World.* London: Zed Books Ltd.

Ramjerdi, Hamideh, and Anthony D'Amato. 1995. "The Intellectual Property Rights Law of the People's Republic of China." *North Carolina Journal of International Law and Commercial Regulation* 21:169-185.

Rapp, Richard, and Richard P. Rozek. 1990a. "Benefits and Costs of Intellectual Property Protection in Developing Countries." *Journal of World Trade* 75/77:75-102.

-- 1990b "Benefits and Costs of Intellectual Property Protection in Developing Countries." National Economic Research Associates, Inc.Working Paper No. 3.

Rawls, John. 1971. *A Theory of Justice*. Cambridge: Belknap Press.

United States Trade Representative. 1996. ""Special 301" on Intellectual Property Rights and 1996 Title VII Decisions."

United States Trade Representative. 1999. "USTR Announces Results of Special 301 Annual Review."

Reynolds, John R., and Lauren J. Krivo. 1996. "Change in Societal Technology and Development, 1950-1990." *Social Science Research* 25:95-124.

Richwine, Lisa. 1999. "Gore Seeks to Defuse South Africa AIDS Controversy." Reuters News Service, June 29.

Riskin, Carl. 1995. *China's Political Economy: The Quest for Development Since 1945*. New York: Oxford University Press.

Robinson, Ronald, John Gallagerh, and Alice Denny. 1967. *Africa and the Victorians: The Official Mind of Imperialism*. London: MacMillan.

Rosen, Stuart M., and Gregory Husisian. 1995. "The Ascent of the Intellectual: How the US Moved to Protect American Intellectual Property Rights in China." *International Trade Law and Regulation* 1:54-58.

Schlesinger, Michael N. 1995. "A Sleeping Giant Awakens: The Development of Intellectual Property Law in China." *Journal of Chinese Law* 9:93-140.

Schumpeter, Joseph. 1976. *Capitalism, Socialism and Democracy*. London: Allen and Unwin.

Schwab, S. C. 1994. "The Omnibus Trade and Competitiveness Act of 1988: The End of an Era in US Trade Policy?" Ph.D. Dissertation. Department of Public Administration of the School of Business and Public Management. Washington: George Washington University Press.

Sell, S. 1995. "The Origins of a Trade-Based Approach to Intellectual Property Protection." *Science Communication* 17(2): 163-184.

Sen, Amartya. 1984a. "Goods and People." In *World Hunger and Morality*, eds. William Aiken and Hugh LaFollette. Upper Saddle River NJ: Prentice Hall.

-- 1984b. *Resources, Values, and Development*. Cambidge: Harvard University Press.

-- 1985. *Commodities and Capabilities*. New York: Elsevier Science Publishers.

Seyoum, Belay. 1996. "The Impact of Intellectual Property Rights on Foreign Direct Investment." *Columbia Journal of World Business* 31:51-59.

Sherwood, Robert M. 1990. *Intellectual Property and Economic Development*. Boulder: Westview Press Inc.

--. 1997. "Intellectual Property Systems and Investment Stimulation: The Rating of Systems in Eighteen Developing Countries." *IDEA*. Vol. 37 No. 2: 261-370.

Shisana, Olive. 1997. "New Medicines Bill Will Benefit Consumers. Statement by Dr. Olive Shisana, Director General of Health." Department of Health, South Africa.

Shue, Henry. 1980. *Basic Rights: Subsistence, Affluence, and US Foreign Policy*. Princeton: Princeton University Press.

Silverman, M., M. Lydecker, et al. 1992. *Bad Medicine: The Prescription Drug Industry in the Third World*. Stanford: Stanford University Press.

Siwek, S. E., and H. W. Furchtogott-Roth. 1993. *International Trade in Computer Software*. Westport: Quorum Books.

Simon, Densi Fred. 1989. "China's Drive to Close the Technological Gap: S & T Reform and the Imperative to Catch Up." *The China Quarterly* 119:599-630.

Skrentny, R. 1989. "Raiders of the Golden Arcade." *California Business News* 24: February, 33-42.

Sloan, T. L. 1990. "The 1988 Trade Act and Intellectual Property Cases before the International Trade Commission." *Santa Clara Law Review* 30:293-324.

Smith, B. L. R. 1990. *American Science Policy Since World War II*. Washington: The Brookings Institute.

Spero, J. E. 1977. *The Politics of International Economic Relations*. New York: St. Martin's Press.

Stapleton, Darwin H. 1978. "The Origin of American Railroad Technology, 1825-1840." *Railroad History* 139:65-77.

Subcommittee on Oversights and Investigations of the Committee on Energy and Commerce. 1983. *Unfair Foreign Trade Practices*. Washington: United States House of Representatives.

Swanevelder, J.P., H.G.V Kustner, and A. Vanmiddelkoop. 1998. "The South African HIV Epidemic, Reflected by Nine Provincial Epidemics, 1990-1996." *South African Medical Journal* 88:1320-1325.

Todaro, Michael P. 1994. *Economic Development, 5th edition*. New York: Longman.

Townsand, James R., and Brantly Womack. 1986. *Politics in China, 3rd Ed.*. Boston: Little, Brown and Company.

United States Code. 1974. Congressional and Administrative News. 93rd Congress, Second Session, Trade Act of 1974. St. Paul: West Publishing. 4:7186+.

United States Congress, Office of Technology Assessment. 1986. Intellectual Property Rights in an Age of Electronic and Information. OTA CIT-302 Washington: US Government Printing Office.

United States State Department. 1999. "US Government Efforts to Negotiate the Repeal, Termination, or Withdrawal of Article 15(c) of the South African Medicines and Related Substances Act of 1965." Washington: United States State Department.

Van Bergeijk, Peter A. G., and Nico W. Mensink. 1997. "Measuring Globalization." *Journal of World Trade* 31:159-168.

Wallace, J., and J. Erickson. 1992. *Hard Drive: Bill Gates and the Making of the Microsoft Corporation*. New Yok: John Wiley & Sons, Inc.

Wasko, J. 1994. *Hollywood in the Information Age: Beyond the Silver Screen*. Austin: University of Texas Press.

Wheaton, J. J. 1986. "Generic Competition and Pharmaceutical Innovation: The Drug Price Competition and Patent Term Restoration Act of 1984." *Catholic University Law Review* 36:433-487.

Wichterman, Dana. 1991. "Intellectual Property Rights and Economic Development: An Issue Brief." Washington: Agency for International Development, Center for Development Information and Evaluation.

Wildman, S. S., and S. E. Siwek. 1988. *International Trade in Films and Television Programs*. Cambridge: Ballinger Publishing Co.

Willard, Geoffrey T. 1996. "An Examination of China's Emerging Intellectual Property Regime: Historical Underpinnings, the Current System and Prospects for the Future." *Indiana International & Comparative Law Review* 6:411-437.

Working Group on Global HIV/AIDS and STD Surveillance. 1998. *South Africa: Epidemiological Fact Sheet on HIV/AIDS and Sexually Transmitted Diseases*. Geneva: UNAIDS World Health Organization.

Wortzel, L. H. 1971. *Technology Transfer in the Pharmaceutical Industry*. Boston: Boston University, UNITAR.

Yergin, D. 1991. *The Prize: The Epic Quest for Oil, Money, and Power*. New York: Simon and Schuster.

Zheng, Henry R. 1987. "The Patent System of the People's Republic of China." *University of San Francisco Law Review* 21:345-392.

Index

Breinigsville, PA USA
08 December 2010
250844BV00002B/7/P

9 781931 202473